MW01715974

Study Guide

for

CHILD DEVELOPMENT:

ITS NATURE AND COURSE

L. Alan Sroufe   Robert G. Cooper

Prepared by

L. Alan Sroufe
University of Minnesota

Everett Waters
State University of New York at Stony Brook

McGRAW-HILL, INC.
New York St. Louis San Francisco Auckland Bogotá Caracas
Hamburg Lisbon London Madrid Mexico Milan Montreal
New Delhi Paris San Juan São Paulo Singapore Sydney
Tokyo Toronto

STUDY GUIDE FOR CHILD DEVELOPMENT

First Edition

987654321

ISBN 0-07-553814-8

PREFACE

Sroufe & Cooper's CHILD DEVELOPMENT: Its Nature and Course is a unique textbook in child psychology. It organizes both the major trends in human development and the details of human social and cognitive growth into a beautifully coherent picture of how we become human and how we become ourselves. The keys to their presentation are clear organization, solid scholarship, and emphasis on principles of development that apply at every age and to every topic. This study guide is designed to help you organize your reading and review, and to help you evaluate your progress through several different types of self-tests.

Psychological research has demonstrated that how people study greatly affects their learning and performance on tests. Each chapter in the Study Guide begins with a list of Learning Objectives. You will learn more from each chapter in the textbook if you read with a purpose, rather than just reading to see what will be on the next page.

Each set of learning goals is followed by a Chapter Summary. The chapter summaries follow the organization of the textbook chapters. They are designed as companions to each textbook chapter, not as substitutes. They focus on key themes and on sections that require special attention. They do not cover every topic in a textbook chapter. These summaries can be useful in two ways. First, understanding and recall are always improved if the reader knows in advance what a textbook chapter is going to be about and how it will unfold. In addition, chapter summaries can be useful guides when you study for a test. It is more effective to re-read a Study Guide summary and look to the text for information that you do not recognize or recall than it is to re-read each textbook chapter before a test. Don't distribute your study time evenly across material you know very well and material that needs more study. Use the study guide to identify material that needs extra time and concentrate your time there.

The chapter summaries are followed by three types of Self-test material, matching, multiple choice, and essay questions. Answers to self-test items and references to specific pages in the textbook are included at the end of each Study Guide chapter. The matching items are designed to test recognition and understanding of concepts that are printed in **boldface** in the textbook. Page numbers indicate where these key terms and concepts appear in the textbook. They are also defined in the glossary at the back of the textbook. The multiple choice questions cover each of the learning objectives listed at the beginning of the Study Guide chapters. They do not cover the full range of questions that you might encounter on a test, but they do allow you to see how material from the textbook might be translated into multiple choice questions.

The sample essay questions are designed to let you practice formulating clear essay answers from material in the textbook. You should write answers of your own in the space provided in the Study Guide, and then compare your answers with the sample answers at the end of the Study Guide chapter. Pay special attention to the way your essay answers are organized. A good essay should show that you (1) understand what is being asked, (2) know the meaning of key terms, (3) can answer the question asked, rather than simply listing every true fact you know about the general topic, and (4) (if you have time) can use examples or apply what you have learned to your own experience.

One of the unique features of CHILD DEVELOPMENT: Its Nature and Course is its integration of the lives of three very real families into the presentation. The families are followed from before the birth of their child through the child's adolescence, in a series of brief episodes or vignettes. One of the goals of your course in child psychology and of the Study Guide as well is to have you relate the material from the textbook chapters to the lives and behavior of people in the real world. In order to accomplish this, the Study Guide includes both multiple choice and essay questions that relate material from the textbook to the vignettes.

Child Development: Its Nature and Course represents an exciting new approach to teaching about human social and cognitive development. It reflects advances in the field of developmental psychology, hundreds of discussions and exchanges with colleagues and students, and years of experience teaching about human development to undergraduates with majors from art history to zoology. We have tried to bring some of this same experience to bear in preparing this Study Guide. We especially appreciate help on each of the Study Guide chapters from German Posada, Keng-Ling Lay, and Suzanne Johnson, graduate students at the State University of New York at Stony Brook.

In the best of all worlds, preparing a study guide would be a continuing process. You can help make subsequent editions even better by sharing any suggestions or critical comments you have. Forward your comments to :

Rochelle Diogenes, Editor
College Division
Random House
201 East 50th Street
New York, NY 10022

CONTENTS

Chapter 1
The Nature of Development

LEARNING OBJECTIVES

When you have studied the material in this chapter, you will be able to:

1. Define qualitative change and behavioral reorganization.
2. Name and describe the key features of developmental change.
3. Define and distinguish between normative and individual development.
4. Describe the factors on which development depends.
5. Give a brief account of Charles Darwin's theory of evolution.
6. Explain the concept of natural selection.
7. Explain the relevance of evolutionary theory to theories of human development.
8. Give examples of interactions between heredity and environment and explain how they influence development.
9. Describe the main characteristics of an experiment and give examples.
10. Distinguish between natural experiments and naturalistic observations.
11. Explain three important research designs used to study change over time.

CHAPTER SUMMARY

(Pp. 3-4) When behavior is studied in context, it becomes more understandable. Development is an important aspect of context. Children differ from one period of development to the next. An older child's capacities emerge in an orderly way from the capacities the child had earlier in life. A person's development is coherent over time. A developmental perspective takes into account the fact that individuals differ from one another.

I. The Concept of Development

A. Development and Behavior **(pp. 4-7)**

Changes in development involve acquiring both new skills and new ways of organizing thoughts and actions. This reorganization results in more complex patterns of behavior. Development during childhood and adolescence involves changes that are orderly, cumulative, and directional.

B. Development, Growth, and Other Changes **(pp. 7-8)**

Development involves both quantitative and qualitative changes. Growth refers to gradual changes that are quantitative in nature. Not all changes children go through are part of their growth or of their development. For example, learning specific skills involves change, but it does not involve developmental change.

C. Normative and Individual Development **(pp. 8-9)**

Normative changes are those that most children go through on the way to adulthood. Individual development refers to variations around the normative course of development. It also refers to the fact that an individual changes with development and yet remains the same person over time.

II. A Framework for Understanding Development

(Pp. 9-10) Three factors account for the processes of development: (1) A preexisting developmental plan built into the organism (genetic potentials), (2) prior development, and (3) supportive environmental conditions (current environmental circumstances).

A. The Darwinian Revolution **(pp. 10-12)**

Charles Darwin proposed an explanation for the diversity of living organisms and their ability to live in different environments. Evolution occurs because individuals who are best suited to survive in a particular environment are most likely to pass their genes on to future generations. One of the most hotly debated questions in biology today is whether evolutionary change is gradual or punctuated by periods of rapid change.

B. Evolutionary Theory and Child Development **(pp. 12-13)**

An evolutionary perspective on child development suggests that what develops is survival-enhancing species-specific behavior. Species-specific behavior is adaptive behavior that is typical of all or most members of a species. Human behaviors frequently have parallels in species related to humans. Evolutionary theory has given an equally important role to both heredity and environment. One cannot be considered without the other.

C. A Viewpoint on Heredity and Environment **(pp. 13-14)**

Most modern child psychologists emphasize that developmental change arises from interactions between heredity and environment. Development depends on both genetic instructions and environmental input and support.

III. Methods for Studying Development

(P. 14). There are many useful approaches to studying human development. Each has advantages and disadvantages. None of the methods discussed in the text is more or less scientific than the others. Whether one method should be preferred over another depends on the question being studied.

A. The Experiment **(pp. 14-16)**

An experiment is a study in which the researcher has a high degree of control over the conditions under which the subjects are observed. Subjects in experiments are randomly assigned to different experimental conditions. Laboratory results do not always apply to real-life settings. Cause-effect relationships demonstrated in the laboratory may not reflect the most common causes of behavior in the outside world. Variables like gender, social class, race, or past experience are difficult to study in true experiments because they cannot be manipulated or assigned to individuals randomly.

B. Observational Methods **(pp. 16-20)**

(Pp. 16-17). Naturalistic observation involves observing behavior as it occurs in everyday contexts. The value of the data is insured by use of precise and systematic methods for observing and recording behavior. Some aspects of behavior are inaccessible to naturalistic observation.

The Natural Experiment **(pp. 17-18).** A natural experiment is a study in which the researcher uses naturally occurring variations or events and examines their effects in order to evaluate a hypothesis. Random assignment of subjects to different conditions is not possible in a natural experiment.

Observing Change Over Time **(pp. 18-20).** Cross-sectional studies examine different groups of people of different ages. Longitudinal studies examine the process of development in a single group of people over time. Longitudinal and cross-sectional methods can be combined in a method called an accelerated longitudinal design. In this method a series of short longitudinal studies is conducted with different groups of subjects, in place of a single long-term study on a single sample.

SELF-TEST

Matching: Key Terms and Concepts

1. ___development is directional (p. 7)
2. ___development is orderly (p. 7)
3. ___individual development (p. 8)
4. ___normative development (p. 8)
5. ___genes (p. 9)
6. ___natural selection (p. 10)
7. ___evolution is punctuated (p. 11)
8. ___species-specific behavior (p. 12)
9. ___experiment (p. 14)
10. ___hypothesis (p. 15)
11. ___ethology (p. 16)
12. ___naturalistic observation (p. 17)
13. ___longitudinal studies (p. 18)
14. ___cross-sectional studies (p. 18)

a. study of species behavior in their natural habitats

b. variations around the average or norm

c. changes follow a logical sequence

d. possible answer to a scientific question

e. study different groups of people at different ages

f. conduct typical of certain species

g. systematic presentation of stimuli

h. follow a group of people for a period of time

i. describes behavior in real life situations

j. study of general changes in behavior across ages

k. Stephen Gould

l. greater complexity in behavioral organization

m. mechanism to explain the adaptation of species

n. contain basic instructions for the unfolding of development

Multiple Choice Questions

1. A developmental perspective includes the idea that people undergo qualitative change. This refers to:

   a. increase in people skills to deal with the world
   b. greater knowledge acquired through experience
   c. fundamental transformations from one period to another
   d. effects of practice on children's behavior
   (Objective 1, Conceptual)

2. Behavioral reorganization refers to:

   a. a new way of putting skills together
   b. a new way of making development coherent over time
   c. the emergence of new skills from old ones
   d. continuity in development
   (Objective 1, Conceptual)

3. Adolescents are able to think of problems in terms of abstract concepts. Younger children are not. This is an example of:

   a. gradual change in development
   b. qualitative change in development
   c. behavioral reorganization in development
   d. quantitative change in knowledge
   (Objective 1, Conceptual)

4. Which of the following refers to the fact that development at any age builds upon accomplishments from preceding ages?

   a. orderly age-related changes
   b. cumulative age-related changes
   c. directional age-related changes
   d. environmental influences on development
   (Objective 2, Conceptual)

5. Development always moves toward greater complexity in behavioral organization. This means that development involves:

   a. orderly age-related changes
   b. cumulative age-related changes
   c. directional age-related changes
   d. quantitative age-related changes
   (Objective 2, Conceptual)

6. Which of the following refers to changes in behavior virtually all children go through?

   a. variations around the average in development
   b. uniqueness of changes children experience
   c. individual differences in children's development
   d. normative changes in development
   (Objective 3, Conceptual)

7. Even though all children become attached to their principal caregiver, some infants are secure and others are anxious in their attachments. These differences are examples of:

   a. normative changes in development
   b. individual development
   c. discontinuity in development
   d. qualitative changes in development
   (Objective 3, Conceptual)

8. Which of the following accounts for the basic blueprint that human development tends to follow?

   a. evolutionary heritage
   b. prior development
   c. immediately preceding changes
   d. supportive environmental conditions
   (Objective 4, Conceptual)

9. Darwin's theory of evolution emphasizes:

   a. that each species is designed for survival in its specific environment
   b. the key role genes play in the survival of the species
   c. that evolutionary change is rapid and abrupt
   d. the superiority of human adaptations
   (Objective 5, Conceptual)

10. What does natural selection result in?

   a. the survival of the strongest individuals
   b. the survival of the species
   c. the survival of some genes and not others
   d. longer lifespan for fitter individuals
   (Objective 6, Conceptual)

11. Evolutionary theory has affected the study of human development by emphasizing that:

a. the human species is unique and unrelated to other species
b. environment determines the changes an individual goes through
c. heredity accounts for the genetic variation within species
d. humans have species-specific behaviors that have adaptive value
(Objective 7, Conceptual)

12. What is illustrated by the fact that negative effects of rubella are much less if it is contracted late in pregnancy?

a. environmental influences determine development
b. genetic influences determine development
c. environmental and genetic influences interact during development
d. development is normal if either genes or the environment is normal
(Objective 8, Conceptual)

13. What are the main advantages of experimental studies on development?

a. validity and sophistication
b. control and precision
c. control and random assignment of subjects
d. validity and random assignment of subjects
(Objective 9, Conceptual)

14. Random assignment of subjects is characteristic of:

a. naturalistic observation studies
b. natural experiments
c. cross-sectional studies
d. laboratory experiments
(Objective 9, Conceptual)

15. Laboratory experiments that do not apply to real-life settings lack:

a. experimental validity
b. precision
c. ecological validity
d. reliability
(Objective 9, Conceptual)

16. Placing a tape recorder under a baby's bed to record sounds it makes when it is alone in the room is an example of:

a. an experiment
b. naturalistic observation
c. a natural experiment
d. a longitudinal study
(Objective 10, Conceptual)

17. A comparison between anxiety levels in a group of children whose neighborhood is plagued by crime and a group from a similar neighborhood with lower crime rates is an example of:

    a. a cross-sectional study
    b. a longitudinal study
    c. a natural experiment
    d. naturalistic observation
    (Objective 10, Conceptual)

18. Longitudinal studies are useful when the researcher's goal is to:

    a. examine the general process of development
    b. examine individual variations in development
    c. show how children go through phases of development
    d. all of the above
    (Objective 11, Conceptual)

19. A cross-sectional study compares different groups of people at different ages. This is a useful way to:

    a. examine variables that influence developmental change
    b. examine individual variations in development
    c. show how quickly children go through phases of development
    d. map out the general course of development
    (Objective 11, Conceptual)

20. A research project on aggression follows three groups of children during three years. The first group consists of three-year-old children, the second of six-year-old children, and the third of nine-year-old children. What type of research design is this?

    a. a longitudinal study
    b. a cross-sectional study
    c. an accelerated longitudinal study
    d. an accelerated cross-sectional study
    (Objective 11, Conceptual)

ESSAY QUESTIONS

1. Development depends upon (1) a pre-existing developmental plan, (2) prior development, and (3) supportive environmental conditions. Briefly describe what these three contributors to development involve **(p. 9).**

2. Summarize the advantages and disadvantages of studying development experimentally **(pp. 14-16).**

ANSWER KEYS

Matching

1. l 2. c 3. b 4. j 5. n 6. m 7. k 8. f 9. g 10. d

11. a 12. i 13. h 14. e

Multiple Choice

1. c (p. 3-6)	11. d (p. 12)
2. a (p. 6)	12. c (p. 13)
3. b (p. 7)	13. b (p. 15)
4. b (p. 7)	14. d (p. 15)
5. c (p. 7)	15. c (p. 15)
6. d (p. 8)	16. b (p. 16)
7. b (p. 8-9)	17. c (p. 17-18)
8. a (p. 9)	18. d (p. 18-19)
9. a (p. 10)	19. d (p. 19)
10. c (p. 10)	20. c (p. 20)

Essay Questions

1. The preexisting plan for development is carried in the genes all humans have in common. But this is not enough to guarantee that an individual will develop normally through the entire course of development. At each point in development, success depends in part on development that has taken place previously. For example, if vision fails to develop properly at an early age, this can have a negative effect on social and cognitive development at later points. A supportive environment is essential for normal expression of our genetic endowment. Even if a child has completely normal genes for vision, it will not develop proper eyesight if it is raised in the dark or is not properly nourished. A supportive environment can help overcome problems related to genetic abnormalities or earlier development, but it may not be enough to overcome them completely.

2. Experiments offer the advantages of control and precision. In the laboratory we expose subjects to stimuli in order to observe their effects on behavior. This has the advantage of allowing us to control exactly what the subject is exposed to. In an experiment, subjects are randomly assigned to groups that will be exposed to different stimuli. Random assignment allows us to be sure that any differences we see between the groups after the stimuli are presented must be due to the stimuli alone. Randomly composed groups would not differ for any other reason. One limitation of experiments is that people may not behave the same way in the laboratory as in the real world. Another potential problem is that stimuli that are studied in the laboratory may not actually be very common in the real world. In such a case, experiments could cause us to make mistakes about which stimuli are the most important causes of some behavior. Experiments that do not translate to the real world very well lack ecological validity.

Chapter 2
Theories of Development

LEARNING OBJECTIVES

When you have studied the material in this chapter, you will be able to:

1. Distinguish between perspectives that have emphasized biological and environmental influences on human development.
2. Explain what a theory is and what a theory is useful for.
3. Identify and describe the basic concepts and developmental stages included in Freud's psychoanalytic theory of development.
4. Identify and describe the course of development suggested by Erikson.
5. Identify and describe the basic concepts and developmental stages included in Piaget's theory of cognitive development.
6. Describe John Bowlby's adaptational theory of infant-parent attachment.
7. Identify and describe the basic concepts of social learning theory.
8. Describe two different information-processing approaches to cognitive development.
9. Summarize the advantages and limitations of major theories of social and cognitive development.

CHAPTER SUMMARY

(Pp. 23-24) A theory of development offers a framework for organizing scientific information. The goal is to present a cohesive view of our knowledge about human development and suggest something about how development occurs. Theories also identify domains that deserve or require further study.

I. Background for Modern Theories of Development

A. Historical Viewpoints on Heredity and Environment **(pp. 24-25)**

John Locke viewed the human infant as a blank slate (tabula rasa). Children are neither good nor bad by nature, but become so by virtue of their environments. Jean Rousseau saw development as a process that occurs by maturation rather than environment. Modern theorists see roles for both inborn and environmental factors in development.

B. The Common Core of Contemporary Positions **(p. 26)**

Psychological and biological processes are influenced by both genetics and environment. Developmental theories also assume that human beings are active organisms. This has two meanings. Human infants are active participants in their own experiences, and they are active in creating their own environment.

C. Continuing Theoretical Diversity **(pp. 26-28)**

Modern developmental theorists differ in the roles they assign to heredity and environment, and in their descriptions of how these factors interact. These differences are not easily resolved, because genetic endowments, environments, and some of our most important human characteristics are very difficult to measure. Agreement exists on the most basic assumption: Human development is influenced by both heredity and environment.

II. The Role of Theory

(Pp. 28-29) Theories of development are intended to explain what we know about development and to predict new observations. Theories also indicate what questions are important to ask and how to ask them. In child development no one theory prevails, because a given set of facts can be interpreted in different ways.

III. Theories Used in the Study of Children

(Pp. 29-30) A developmentally oriented theory is one that explicitly emphasizes the orderly, cumulative, and directional changes in children and their behavior over time.

A. Major Developmental Theories **(pp. 30-40)**

Psychoanalytic Views **(pp. 30-32).** Freud's theory of psychological development evolved from his ideas about the causes of emotional problems. His theory of development focuses on primitive drives and instincts (the Id), the self (Ego), and the conscience (Superego). His theory of motivation placed great emphasis on the desire to satisfy biological needs such as hunger and thirst. Freud proposed five stages of development: oral, anal, phallic, latency, and genital. Frustration or failure to get sufficient drive gratification in any of these stages could result in the person's becoming locked (fixated) in that particular psychological mode of conflict.

Psychoanalysts since Freud have considerably expanded the concept of the ego. For example, Erik Erikson proposed a theory of ego development that involved facing and resolving a series of important developmental tasks. The issues Erikson emphasized are: basic trust vs. mistrust; autonomy vs. shame and doubt; initiative vs. guilt; industry vs. inferiority; identity vs. role confusion; intimacy vs. isolation; generativity vs. stagnation; and ego integrity vs. despair.

Piagetian Developmental Theory **(pp. 32-38).** The Swiss psychologist Jean Piaget discovered that children view and think about the world in very different ways at different stages of development. He identified three major periods in cognitive development. Cognitive structures are basic ways of thinking that underlie and organize the child's activities. Cognitive structures are different at each stage of development. All children progress through the three periods in the same order. The age boundaries for each stage are approximate. The order is essential.

The sensorimotor period extends from birth to 2 years of age. It is called the sensorimotor period because the infant understands the world through perceptual (sensory) and action (motor) systems. At this stage children understand objects primarily in terms of the behaviors or skills that they can apply to them.

The concrete period goes from age 2 through age 11. Piaget divided this period into the preoperational subperiod (2 to 7 years of age) and the concrete operational subperiod (7 to 11 years of age). In the preoperational subperiod skills are acquired independently of one another. In the concrete operational period skills are organized into a system of logical thinking that expands the child's cognitive capabilities.

The formal period extends from about twelve years of age through adulthood. The child is able to reason systematically about hypothetical problems and abstract issues.

Piaget used the term adaptation too describe the process of change. Adaptation occurs through assimilation and accommodation. Assimilation is the tendency to act on or to interpret the world through existing schemes or structures. Accommodation is the tendency to modify schemes or structures to conform to aspects of the environment. The process of going from a state of disequilibrium to new and more serviceable structures is called equilibration.

Bowlby's Adaptational Theory **(pp. 38-40)**. The British psychiatrist John Bowlby has proposed that the human infant's tendency to become attached to available adults is based on biases in human infants' learning abilities that are part of our evolutionary heritage. Despite his emphasis on the biological foundations of the capacity to form attachments, Bowlby affirms that the quality of those attachments is heavily influenced by the quality of care the baby has.

Bowlby argued that by the end of the first year the infant has developed internal working models of self and other. These models are expectations about the caregiver as available and responsive or unavailable and unresponsive, and complementary expectations about the self as worthy or unworthy of care. Secure attachment involves confidence in the caretaker's availability and responsiveness. Attachment models influence many aspects of personality development, especially the growth of self-reliance. Bowlby rejected Freud's concepts of drive gratification, infantile sexuality, and fixation.

B. Other Influential Theories **(pp. 40-46)**

(Pp. 40-41) Some theorists have emphasized continuous rather than stagelike change in their developmental models.

Social Learning Theory **(pp. 41-44)**. Social learning theory has its origins in behaviorism. Behaviorism emphasizes the study of observable behavior learned through associations. Positive reinforcement involves receiving a reward after performing a specific behavior. Negative reinforcement occurs when an unpleasant stimulus is removed after a specific behavior is performed. Negative reinforcement increases the likelihood of the behavior being repeated. It should not be confused with punishment. Punishment refers to the presentation of a negative event after some behavior to affect the child's behavior. Shaping refers to the process of learning elaborate sequences of behavior bit by bit, through careful application of punishment and reinforcement.

Social learning theorists place special emphasis on cognitive activity that occurs during the learning process. For example, Albert Bandura has emphasized the importance of observation and vicarious rewards and punishments. Children clearly learn many behaviors by observing others. They are also encouraged to try or discouraged from trying new behaviors when they see that others are rewarded or punished for them.

Information-Processing Theory **(pp. 44-46)**. Information-processing theory is an approach to understanding human problem solving, memory, decision making, concept formation, and other complex behaviors. Information-processing theory attempts to detail the cognitive and behavioral steps involved in performing a task or solving a problem. Much like a computer, a person can be viewed as receiving raw information, processing and extracting meaning, and then selecting and applying rules or procedures that produce a final output.

Researchers who employ an information-processing approach have suggested several explanations for developmental change. Robert Siegler suggested that as children grow older they are capable of performing a wider array of operations on the information they take. Robbie Case explained important aspects of cognitive development in terms of increased capacity in the child's working memory system. Working memory is where we hold the perceptions, images, and concepts we are actively using at any given moment. Klahr and Wallace proposed that the human information-processing system is organized into three subsystems: input, goal-setting, and planning and learning. The input subsystem refers to perception and attention. The learning subsystem refers to the mental operations a person can perform, and it is the most important in reference to development since it enables acquisition of new thinking and problem solving strategies. The information-processing perspective can also be used to study social development.

C. Comparing Theories **(pp. 46-49)**

Different theories of development help explain different aspects of development. Each has limitations. Freud's theory can be criticized for emphasizing negative motivations, and for relying on difficult concepts. Piaget's theory can be criticized for concentrating almost exclusively on cognitive factors without considering emotional ones. Bowlby's theory has not yet been fully tested and is more an outline for a theory than a fully detailed theory. Social learning theory sees development in a relatively narrow focus and gives the impression that each behavior is learned in isolation. Information-processing theory does not give enough importance to human motivations and some of its concepts have not been demonstrated through research.

SELF-TEST

Matching: Key Terms and Concepts

1.___John Locke (p. 24)
2.___Jean Rousseau (p. 25)
3.___theory (p. 28)
4.___repression (p. 30)
5.___psychoanalysis (p. 30)
6.___pleasure principle (p. 31)
7.___fixation (p. 31)
8.___assimilation (p. 37)
9.___accommodation (p. 37)
10.___internal working model (p. 39)
11.___Ivan Pavlov (p. 41)
12.___negative reinforcement (p. 42)
13.___punishment (p. 42)
14.___Albert Bandura (p. 42)
15.___algorithm (p. 45)

a. action on or interpretation of the world through existing schemes
b. classical conditioning
c. rule
d. infant as tabula rasa
e. form of therapy
f. removal of an unpleasant stimulus
g. observational learning
h. a set of assumptions about how things operate
i. alteration of structures to conform with environment
j. human development unfolds naturally, in positive ways
k. pushing traumatic memories into the unconscious
l. generalized expectations of the caregiver and of self
m. desire to satisfy biological needs
n. presentation of aversive stimulus
o. being locked in a particular developmental stage

Multiple Choice Questions

1. Which theorist proposed that children become good or bad by virtue of the types of experience they have?

   a. Darwin
   b. Locke
   c. Rousseau
   d. Freud
   (Objective 1, Conceptual)

2. What did Rousseau suggest as the main force(s) promoting development?

   a. maturation
   b. environment
   c. maturation and environment
   d. neither maturation nor environment
   (Objective 1, Conceptual)

3. If children are active organisms from the very beginning of development, then they are also:

   a. the product of an active environment
   b. changeable organisms that depend on the environment
   c. partly responsible for creating their own environments
   d. the product of genetic factors
   (Objective 1, Conceptual)

4. A theory refers to:

   a. observations that help to design new studies
   b. observations and predictions about development
   c. a framework for interpreting facts and guiding research
   d. a framework of guesses about how things work
   (Objective 2, Conceptual)

5. Which part of the mind did Freud say consists of primitive drives and instincts?

a. unconscious
b. superego
c. ego
d. id
(Objective 3, Conceptual)

6. What part of the mind did Freud assign the role of finding safe and appropriate ways for the drives and instincts to be expressed?

a. unconscious
b. superego
c. ego
d. id
(Objective 3, Conceptual)

7. Freud suggested that failure to experience drive gratification could result in the person becoming locked in a particular stage of psychological functioning. This is what he called:

a. identification
b. repression
c. fixation
d. frustration
(Objective 3, Conceptual)

8. Freud saw the confrontation of frightening or painful events as a way to cope with and overcome our negative emotions. He referred to this as:

a. the mastery motive
b. the pleasure principle
c. the process of conscience
d. anxiety
(Objective 3, Conceptual)

9. Which is the first stage in Freud's theory of development?

a. oral stage
b. phallic stage
c. genital stage
d. anal stage
(Objective 3, Conceptual)

10. Erikson's theory emphasizes

a. satisfaction of biological needs
b. the pleasure principle as active
c. the id as the main force of development
d. the ego as active in mastering experience
(Objective 4, Conceptual)

11. Which psychologist is noted for his theory of cognitive development?

a. Freud
b. Erikson
c. Bowlby
d. Piaget
(Objective 5, Factual)

12. In which order do children progress through the Piagetian stages of cognitive development?

a. concrete, sensorimotor, formal
b. sensorimotor, concrete, formal
c. formal, concrete, sensorimotor
d. concrete, formal, sensorimotor
(Objective 5, Conceptual)

13. During which Piagetian stage does the child understand or know the world mainly through perception and action ?

a. formal operational
b. concrete preoperational
c. sensorimotor
d. concrete operational
(Objective 5, Conceptual)

14. The central achievement that distinguishes Piaget's preoperational subperiod from the sensorimotor period is the ability to:

a. act upon concrete things
b. form mental representations of things
c. think logically about concrete things
d. understand basic quantitative concepts
(Objective 5, Conceptual)

15. In the concrete operational subperiod the child is able to:

a. perform certain logical operations on objects
b. perform certain logical operations at the level of ideas
c. think abstractly about concepts such as justice
d. all of the above
(Objective 5, Conceptual)

16. What did Piaget say sensorimotor infants use to know and act upon the world?

    a. schemes
    b. adaptations
    c. assimilations
    d. equilibrations

    (Objective 5, Conceptual)

17. The evolution of new and more serviceable structures that allow the child to face experiences that previously were not easily assimilated is referred to as the process of:

    a. disequilibrium
    b. adaptation
    c. reflective abstraction
    d. equilibration

    (Objective 5, Conceptual)

18. Bowlby explains the fact that most infants become attached to their primary caregivers by hypothesizing that the infant:

    a. associates its parents with the satisfaction of biological needs
    b. is disposed to become attached by its evolutionary heritage
    c. is reinforced by interacting with its parents
    d. has a working model of the parents

    (Objective 6, Conceptual)

19. Classical conditioning involves creating an association between:

    a. two stimuli
    b. a stimulus and a response
    c. a response and a consequence
    d. a response and a reinforcement

    (Objective 7, Conceptual)

20. Negative reinforcement refers to

    a. punishment
    b. a negative event that follows a behavior
    c. the removal of an unpleasant event
    d. all of the above

    (Objective 7, Conceptual)

21. A child watches a peer giving away his crayons and being praised for that act. Later on this child does the same with her crayons. This is an example of:

a. positive reinforcement
b. observational learning
c. shaping
d. negative reinforcement
(Objective 7, Conceptual)

22. Social learning theorists stress the importance of:

a. cognitive factors during the learning process
b. reinforcer events during the process of learning
c. observing others in learning
d. practical experience during the learning process
(Objective 7, Factual)

23. Siegler proposes that when children grow older they become able to perform a wider range of operations on the information they take in. The most important among these operations are certain procedures called:

a. chunking strategies
b. inputs
c. setting goals
d. heuristics
(Objective 8, Conceptual)

24. A college student has to learn and repeat nine letters within a limited period of time. The letters are: N B C A B C C B S. In order to accomplish the task the student forms three groups: NBC, ABC, and CBS. This is an example of:

a. algorithm
b. heuristics
c. working memory
d. chunking
(Objective 8, Conceptual)

ESSAY QUESTIONS

1. A theory is an organized set of assumptions about how things operate. Describe the role of a theory, and the characteristics by which it could be evaluated.

2. Freud, Bowlby, Piaget, social learning theorists, and information-processing theorists have offered theories that help explain various aspects of development. Briefly describe the key limitations of each theory.

ANSWER KEYS

Matching

1. d	2. j	3. h	4. k	5. e	6. m	7. o	8. a
9. i	10. l	11. b	12. f	13. n	14. g	15. c	

Multiple Choice

1. b (p. 25)	13. c (p. 34)
2. a (p. 25)	14. b (p. 35)
3. c (p. 26)	15. a (p. 37)
4. c (p. 28)	16. d (p. 37)
5. d (p. 31)	17. d (p. 37)
6. c (p. 31)	18. b (p. 38)
7. c (p. 31)	19. a (p. 41)
8. a (p. 31)	20. c (p. 42)
9. a (p. 33)	21. b (p. 42)
10. d (p. 32)	22. a (p. 42)
11. d (p. 32)	23. d (p. 45)
12. b (p. 35)	24. d (p. 45)

Essay Questions

1. A theory provides a framework for interpreting facts and findings. It attempts to account for current observations and to predict future ones. Observations take on meaning when interpreted on the basis of some theory. A theory also serves to guide research. It helps researchers to decide which questions are important to ask, which issues are important to study. A theory must be sensible, plausible, and consistent. It must also organize, integrate and make coherent the body of research findings. A theory must be specific and testable **(pp. 28-29).**

2. Freud's theory can be criticized for emphasizing negative motivations, and for relying on difficult concepts. Piaget's theory can be criticized for concentrating almost exclusively on cognitive factors without considering emotional ones. Bowlby's theory has not yet been fully tested and in addition is too sketchy. Social learning theory sees development in a relatively narrow focus and gives the impression that each behavior is learned in isolation. Information-processing theory does not give enough importance to human motivations and some of its concepts have not been demonstrated through research **(p. 49).**

Chapter 3
The Contexts of Development

LEARNING OBJECTIVES

When you have studied the material in this chapter, you will be able to:

1. Name the important contexts within which development occurs.
2. Describe and explain the biological context of development.
3. Describe and explain the immediate environmental context of development.
4. Describe and explain the social and economic context of development.
5. Explain the relevance of poverty for child development.
6. Explain the relevance of different settings outside the family for human development.
7. Describe and explain the cultural context of development.
8. Describe and explain early development as a context of later development.
9. Explain how the different contexts in which development occurs interact.

CHAPTER SUMMARY

(Pp. 57-60) Physical and psychological development in humans need an appropriate context to happen. If the context is abnormal, development may be so. It is very difficult to say whether or not the effects of early environmental deprivation are reversible in any particular case. But it is clear that the context in which a child grows strongly influences the child's development.

I. An Overview of the Contexts

(Pp. 60-61) Human evolutionary history is part of the context in which human development occurs. The contexts for development also include culture and subculture, the particular period of history, the community, the family, and the immediate surroundings of the child. Bronfenbrenner has suggested a model involving 1) the immediate environment, which refers to all the settings, people, and physical objects with which the child has direct contact, 2) the social and economic context, which refers to the broader context in which the immediate environment is embedded, and 3) the cultural context, which refers to all beliefs, values, and guidelines for behavior that people in a particular society tend to share.

II. The Biological Context

(Pp. 61-64) A child's evolutionary heritage consists of certain traits shared by mammals, others shared only among primates, and others exclusively characteristic of humans. This heritage includes a precise timetable for the appearance of many developmental milestones.

A strong disposition to act on the environment is one of the most basic of all the biological givens in humans. Humans also inherit predispositions to learn and be social. Biologically based variation within a species is an important factor in the species' ability to meet environmental challenges. Biologically based differences among individuals affect development both directly and indirectly.

Canalization refers to genetic constraints on how much the environment can influence particular capacities. Some capacities are strongly canalized, others are easier to change with environmental variations. Some capacities are strongly canalized early in life and the constraints become more rigid with age; others are strongly canalized early in life but they become more changeable in response to environmental change with age.

III. The Child's Immediate Environment

A. The Influence of Objects on Development **(p. 65)**

Children learn by doing. They are especially attracted to objects that respond to them. The pace of cognitive development is strongly affected by the responsiveness of people and objects in a child's environment.

B. The Family Context **(pp. 65-73)**

The family is a dominant part of the child's immediate environment. Family members stimulate development, provide models for important social behaviors and social roles, and provide the child with the security of nurturing relationships.

The Family as a System **(pp. 66-69).** A mothers' infant care practices are strongly influenced by the behavior of other family members. The child itself also plays an important part in shaping the type of care it receives. The family is an interconnected system of relationships, not a set of separate relationships.

Viewing the family as a system implies that influence between the members of the system moves in two directions. Parental behavior shapes children's responses, which in turn modify parental behavior. Sameroff emphasizes that individuals, their contexts, and their two-way interactions are all important in explaining developmental outcomes.

Fathers in the Family System **(pp. 69-71).** Fathers have both direct and indirect effects on their children. Child-father attachment is evident early in development. Mothers and fathers behave differently towards their children. Marital harmony is associated with parental well-being, nurturant parenting, and child adjustment. Research on father absence, divorce, and related topics indicates that, during middle childhood, boys from father-absent homes are less oriented to contact sports, less competitive, and more dependent.

Siblings in the Family System **(pp. 71-73).** Siblings too, have direct and indirect effects on children. Direct effects include acting as companions, teachers, and models. Siblings may indirectly influence children's development through their arrival and through the impact they have on their parents' behavior. Birth order may also affect a child's behavior and development.

IV. The Social and Economic Context

A. Family Changes and Social-Economic Factors **(pp. 73-77)**

Some changes in the family are due to social and economic forces in which it is embedded.

Single Parenting and Its Effects **(pp. 74-76).** Children of unmarried teenage mothers frequently encounter developmental problems. Yet, since these mothers often have low incomes, it may be the stresses of being poor rather than the mother's age that accounts for some of the problems these children encounter. The effects of single parenting can be indirect. Having children alone may bring financial difficulties, which in turn can cause stresses and child-rearing problems.

Children often experience negative effects if their parents divorce. But divorce is not always a devastating experience to children. The effects depend on many factors. Short-term effects appear to be more serious for boys; effects on gender behavior and social relationships may subtly persist. There may also be long-term effects if, as often occurs, the custodial parent experiences a sharp decline in income.

Maternal Employment and Its Effects **(pp. 76-77).** The effects of maternal employment on children's development depend on the child's age and gender, the amount of time the mother spends at work, the quality of shared time remaining, the quality of substitute care, the security of the parent-child relationship, and the mother's view of the work as stressful or rewarding.

B. Social Class, Poverty, and Stress **(pp. 77-79)**

Families from different social and economic classes have many things in common in their child-rearing practices. They also show many important differences. Children of poor families are more likely to suffer prenatal problems, poor physical health at birth, and death during infancy than children of middle class families. Crowded conditions, financial uncertainty, and general instability in life circumstances are stresses associated with poverty. Children of poor families are more likely to have behavioral and emotional problems, to drop out of school, to be labeled learning disabled, and to spend time in a correctional institution as adolescents than children of middle-class families.

C. Social Settings Outside the Family **(pp. 79-83)**

The Day-Care Setting **(pp. 79-80).** Many families requiring child-care services make informal arrangements such as having several children cared for in someone else's home. Other families use organized day-care centers. We need a great deal more information about the potential costs and benefits of different types of day-care arrangements.

The Peer Group **(pp. 80-81).** According to Hartup, the child's peer group is second only to the family in its influence on development. Peer influence increases with age. The peer group teaches the child how to interact in symmetrical relationships. Children also learn cultural norms and values from their peers.

The School **(pp. 81-82).** The school is the child's work place. School activities vary with a child's age. Whether school is more a positive or a negative influence on development depends substantially on how the school is run and how teachers interact with students.

V. The Cultural Context

A. Cultural Influences **(pp. 84-85)**

Human development is shaped by a society's culture. Culture also shapes values that a child is taught and exposed to. Anthropologists believe that cultural differences are adaptations to the circumstances in which people live.

B. Cultural Change and Child Development **(pp. 86-87)**

Cultural changes affect both parenting and child development. Ideas about raising children change as a result of technological progress and also in response to fashion and social movements.

C. Subcultures **(p. 87)**

Within a society, some groups adhere to norms and values that differ somewhat from those of the dominant culture. These groups are called subcultures.

VI. Development as Context

(Pp. 87-89) Development itself is a context for further development. It gives each person a developmental history that influences future development. It also provides a context for future development by changing children physically and psychologically through the process of maturation.

VII. Contexts in Interaction

(P. 89) Human development occurs within a set of contexts. None of the contexts seen so far exists in isolation, and none exerts its influence apart from the others. All contexts interact and help to shape the child's development. An important point to keep in mind about developmental contexts is that certain environmental factors tend to go together. Another point to remember is that all the environmental influences seen are funneled to some extent through the family. Biological, socioeconomic, and cultural factors provide the challenges parents face and the resources they may use for rearing their child.

SELF-TEST

Matching: Key Terms and Concepts

1.___biological context (p. 60)
2.___immediate environment (p. 60)
3.___cultural context (p. 60)
4.___canalization (p. 64)
5.___reciprocal determinism (p. 67)
6.___sensitive care (p. 68)
7.___social class (p. 77)
8.___physical discipline (p. 77)
9.___discipline by reasoning (p. 77)
10.___poverty is related to (p. 78)
11.___family day care (p. 79)
12.___symmetrical relationship (p. 81)
13.___school (p. 81)
14.___subculture (p. 87)
15.___maturation (p. 88)

a. low adjustment in children
b. bidirectional effects
c. middle class
d. peer group
e. evolutionary history
f. child's workplace
g. beliefs and values
h. informal care arrangement
i. genetic constraints
j. family
k. working class
l. mother's fitting her behavior to child's needs
m. group with values that differ from those of the dominant group
n. determined by social and economic factors
o. process by which development provides context for development

Multiple Choice Questions

1. Which of the following has proposed a model of developmental contexts and the general way they interact.?

   a. Sameroff
   b. Bronfenbrenner
   c. Sroufe
   d. Gould
   (Objective 1, Factual)

2. Which developmental context is represented by our common human evolutionary heritage?

   a. biological
   b. social and economic
   c. cultural
   d. immediate
   (Objective 2, Conceptual)

3. Which of the following would be included in the biological context of development?

   a. the tendency to attend to human speech sounds
   b. the disposition to act on the environment
   c. the predisposition to form bonds
   d. all of the above
   (Objective 2, Factual)

4. Which aspect of a species' evolutionary heritage helps it to adapt to new or changing environmental demands?

   a. biological influences at the level of the species
   b. individual variation within the species
   c. same genetic makeup in different generations
   d. canalization
   (Objective 2, Factual)

5. Which context of development do parents, peers, and teachers contribute to?

   a. social and economic
   b. educational
   c. immediate
   d. cultural
   (Objective 3, Conceptual)

6. Aggression by husbands against wives is associated with low-quality maternal care for the children in the family. What does this illustrate?

a. bidirectional effects
b. reciprocal determinism
c. fathers' indirect effects
d. mothers' indirect effects
(Objective 3, Conceptual)

7. Sameroff's transactional model describes:

a. long-term bidirectional effects of parents and child
b. indirect effects of parents on the child
c. direct effects of parents on the child
d. short-term bidirectional effects of parents and child
(Objective 3, Factual)

8. Which concept is related to the idea that individuals in a family are fundamentally changed by the organization of the whole family?

a. developmental context
b. system
c. transactional model
d. all of the above
(Objective 3, Factual)

9. Fathers' influences on child development are evident in:

a. fathers' effect on mothers' behavior toward the infant
b. the differences in development between children in intact homes and children in father-absent homes
c. the fact that parents behave differently toward children when father and mother are together
d. all of the above
(Objective 3, Conceptual)

10. Research on the influence of siblings on development has shown that siblings:

a. serve as teachers and models
b. make children more competitive
c. increase the level of conflict in the family
d. all of the above
(Objective 3, Factual)

11. Which context of development includes the effects of both maternal employment and peer groups?

    a. biological
    b. immediate
    c. cultural
    d. social and economic

    (Objective 4, Conceptual)

12. Which of the following might explain the fact that children of unmarried teenage mothers encounter high rates of developmental problems?

    a. financial stress
    b. absence of social support
    c. child-rearing difficulties
    d. all of the above

    (Objective 4, Factual)

13. The influences of maternal employment on child development are complicated. Perhaps the most significant factor is the:

    a. quality of substitute care
    b. meaning of woman's employment for both her and her husband
    c. amount of time the mother spends at work
    d. quality of shared time remaining

    (Objective 4, Factual)

14. Which of the following is most directly associated with prenatal problems and later psychological adjustment problems?

    a. maternal employment
    b. single parenting
    c. divorce
    d. poverty

    (Objective 5, Factual)

15. Poverty is associated with school failure. This limits job opportunities and thus maintains poverty. This combination of effects is called:

    a. poverty's self-perpetuating trap
    b. poverty's low adjustment outcomes
    c. poverty's negative community conditions
    d. poverty's unstable conditions

    (Objective 5, Conceptual)

16. What type of day care arrangement is involved when a child receives care from individual baby-sitters in the child's own home?

a. formal day-care arrangement
b. family day-care arrangement
c. informal arrangement
d. this is not day care
(Objective 6, Conceptual)

17. Which of the following is second only to the family in its impact on development?

a. day-care setting
b. peer group
c. school
d. social context
(Objective 6, Factual)

18. Which of the following is an important source of information about how to behave in symmetrical relationships?

a. family
b. day-care setting
c. peer group
d. school
(Objective 6, Factual)

19. Which of the following contexts includes the values and norms that people in a particular society share?

a. biological
b. immediate
c. social and economic
d. cultural
(Objective 7, Conceptual)

20. Cultural influences shape:

a. the structure of the developmental settings
b. universal set of values in children
c. differences in people's behavior within a culture
d. all of the above
(Objective 7, Factual)

21. Which of the following groups is an example of a subculture within our society?

    a. Chicanos
    b. office workers
    c. women
    d. children

    (Objective 7, Conceptual)

22. Which term refers to previous experiences and aspects of one's developmental history that influence the course of subsequent development?

    a. immediate context of development
    b. maturation
    c. biological context of development
    d. development as context

    (Objective 8, Factual)

23. Which of the following is most influenced by maturation?

    a. culture
    b. social and economic status
    c. physical and cognitive development
    d. knowledge of specific skills

    (Objective 8, Conceptual)

24. Peter and Joan are happily married, are satisfied with their jobs, and enjoy the support of their relatives. They provide their daughter with good-quality care and she does not have any developmental problem so far. This is an illustration of:

    a. the importance of cultural factors for development
    b. the fact that certain environmental factors tend to go together
    c. the importance of the immediate context for development
    d. the fact that social support affects children's outcomes

    (Objective 9, Conceptual)

ESSAY QUESTIONS

1. Explain two ways in which development itself provides a context for further development. Give an example of each.

2. Give an example of a birth-order effect on development and explain what might cause this effect.

ANSWER KEYS

Matching

1. e 2. j 3. g 4. i 5. b 6. l 7. n 8. k 9. c 10. a
11. h 12. d 13. f 14. m 15. o

Multiple Choice

1. b (p. 60)	13. b (p. 76)
2. a (p. 61)	14. d (p. 78)
3. d (pp. 61-62)	15. a (p. 78)
4. b (p. 63)	16. c (p. 79)
5. c (p. 64)	17. b (p. 80)
6. c (p. 69)	18. c (p. 81)
7. a (p. 67)	19. d (p. 83)
8. b (p. 68)	20. a (p. 84)
9. d (pp. 69-70)	21. a (p. 87)
10. a (p. 71)	22. d (p. 87)
11. d (pp. 76, 80)	23. c (p. 88)
12. d (p. 75)	24. b (p. 89)

Essay Questions

1. Development gives each person a set of expectations and ways of dealing with new demands. These influence the course of later development. The development of secure attachment in infancy leaves the child with a sense of self-confidence, which can serve him or her well in the preschool period. Development also provides a context for future development by changing children both physically and intellectually through the process of maturation. These changes have a dramatic influence on the way children interact with their environments. For example, toddlers begin to understand and use language as a result of cognitive maturation. This widens the array of possibilities parents have to influence their children, and also the ways children have to interact with the world **(pp. 87-88)**.

2. First-born children tend to be more motivated toward achievement than later-borns. Many factors contribute to this. One may be the fact that parents' attention is more completely available when they have only one child. When they have a second or later child, their attention must be divided among several children. As a result, later-borns may receive less consistent encouragement toward achievement. Parents also tend to adopt a more relaxed attitude in rearing later-borns **(p. 72)**.

Chapter 4
Heredity and Prenatal Development

LEARNING OBJECTIVES

When you have studied the material in this chapter, you will be able to:

1. Name and describe key general processes in prenatal development.
2. Explain what genes and chromosomes are.
3. Describe the key steps in cell division and how a great variety of gene combinations is achieved in the process.
4. Describe the course of prenatal gender development.
5. Describe how genes interact with one another.
6. Describe the process of conception.
7. Name the three major periods of prenatal development and describe their major characteristics.
8. Explain what a teratogen is and identify basic teratogenic factors.
9. Identify different procedures for detection of fetal problems.
10. Describe familiar birth complications and general trends in childbirth.
11. Explain how the environmental context influences prenatal development.

CHAPTER SUMMARY

(Pp. 93-94) Genes help to guide development, but they can function only within appropiate environmental conditions. Differentiation and reorganization are key processes in prenatal development. Like all human development, prenatal development is orderly, cumulative, and directional.

I. Genes, Heredity, and Evolution

(Pp. 94-95) Evolution has established certain limitations and certain potentials in the human species. Evolutionary theory explains both diversity among species and diversity within species. Mutations are natural changes in genes that alter the instructions they give. Mutations add to the genetic diversity of a species. Genetic engineering techniques include methods for inducing mutations and for inserting new genes into simple organisms.

A. The Mechanisms of Heredity **(pp. 95-104)**

The human genetic endowment is encoded in 23 pairs of chromosomes. The chromosomes of each pair are called homologous because their genes influence the same aspects of development. Each chromosome is made up of DNA. Genes are segments of DNA on the chromosomes. The sperm and the egg each contain half the number of chromosomes of other body cells.

Mitosis, Meiosis, and Assortment of Genes **(pp. 96-99).** A fertilized human egg contains 46 chromosomes. New cells are formed when the fertilized egg duplicates the chromosomes it contains and then divides into two new cells. This is called mitosis. Both daughter cells are identical until they undergo a process called differentiation and acquire specialized functions appropriate for the organs or tissues they will become. Sperm and egg cells only contain half the number of chromosomes of other cells. They are formed by meiosis. Random assortment of chromosomes during meiosis, and the process of crossing over, result in combinations of genes that are different from both parents.

How Do Genes Influence Development **(p. 100)**? The influence that genes have on development is not strictly written into the DNA on the chromosomes. Much of what a gene does depends on the enviromnment in which it is operating. One key element in a gene's environment is the characteristics and activity of neighboring cells. The genetic environment is also influenced by the organism's developmental history.

The Case of Gender Development **(pp. 100-102).** A child's gender is determined by genes on chromosome pair number 23. Pair 23 consists of two X chromosomes in females; one X and one Y chromosome in males. In the seventh week after conception, the Y chromosome activates the gonad tissue to differentiate into testes. If no Y exists the gonad tissue develops into ovaries. Hormones influence gender development from here on. Once testes are formed they produce male sex hormones (androgens) which cause the formation of penis and reproductive tract. The absence of male sex hormones is the signal for females sex organs to develop. Female sex hormones (estrogens) activate female sexual maturity and influence secondary sexual characteristics later in development. Thus hormones are part of the environment that affects what genes do and when.

How Genes Affect One Another **(pp. 102-104).** Genes interact not only with their environment, but also with one another. Alternate forms of genes for a trait are called alleles. If a person has the same alleles for a trait, she or he is said to be homozygous for this trait. If a person has two different alleles for a trait, she or he is said to be heterozygous. Traits can be dominant, codominant, or recessive. Dominant traits are those expressed even if the person is heterozygous for a particular trait. If both alleles are dominant, the two are co-dominant; the characteristics both alleles code for will be expressed. Recessive traits are only expressed if the person is homozygous for that trait.

Genotype refers to the particular set of genes a person has. Phenotype refers to a person's observable characteristics. We cannot be sure of the underlying genotype by examining a person's phenotype because different genes can give similar results, and because the environment affects the way genes are expressed. Characteristics that are caused by more than one pair of genes are called polygenic. Modifier genes do not cause specific traits of their own; instead their action serves to modify the activity of other genes.

II. Conception

A. Events Leading Up to Conception **(pp. 104-106)**

In most women, an ovum ripens in one of her ovaries about every 28 days. An ovum that has been united with a sperm cell is called a zygote. Monozygotic twins result when a single fertilized egg divides by mitosis and then one of the new cells separates and begins to develop into a separate individual with the same genes as its cotwin. If two egg cells are released and fertilized, the outcome is dizygotic twins. Dizygotic twins do not have the same genes.

B. Infertility (pp. 106-107)

Couples differ along a continuum of fertility. Some readily conceive children. Many have some difficulty but eventually succeed. Some couples are unable to conceive. Most of the problems of infertility result from physical causes. Medical techniques can often enable infertile couples to conceive children.

III. Prenatal Development

A. The Stages of Prenatal Development (pp. 108-115)

The prenatal period lasts from conception to birth. It is divided into three periods, the germinal period, the embryonic period, and the fetal period.

Germinal Period: Conception to Week 2 (pp. 108-109). During the germinal period the zygote becomes implanted in the lining of the uterus and begins to form the life-support system through which it will obtain nutrients and eliminate wastes until birth. The cluster of cells developing in the uterine wall is called the blastocyst.

Embryonic Period: Weeks 2 Through 8 (pp. 107-112). After the blastocyst is firmly implanted it is called an embryo. During the embryonic period rapid differentiation occurs. Vital organs and other major parts of the body are formed. The support system consists of three parts: the placenta, the umbilical cord, and the amniotic sac. The placenta provides oxygen and nutrients to the embryo and carries away waste products. The placenta filters out some but not all substances that are harmful to the embryo.

By the end of the third week three different types of tissue are formed: endoderm, mesoderm, and ectoderm. Endoderm cells will develop into internal organs. Mesoderm cell will develop into muscles, skeleton, and blood. Ectoderm cell will develop into the central nervous system, sensory organs, and skin. Critical period refers to a limited time during which some part of the organism is susceptible to influences that can cause specific and permanent changes.

Fetal Period: Week 9 to Birth (pp. 112-115). Once all the major organ systems of the body are beginning to develop, the developing organism is called a fetus. The fetal period is a time of rapid growth and refinement. Fetal movements are more organized, regular, and integrated than movements in the embryonic period.

B. Environmental Effects (pp. 115-122)

Environmental factors that can cause abnormal development are called teratogens. The danger of teratogens is generally greatest during the embryonic period, when differentiation and cell specialization are most rapid.

Drugs (pp. 115-119). Moderate to heavy alcohol consumption during pregnancy can result in fetal alcohol syndrome, the symptoms of which include retardation in growth and intellectual development; defects in facial features, limbs, the brain, and internal organs; irritability and short attention span.

Pregnant mothers who smoke are more likely to deliver prematurely and the more they smoke the greater the risk. Babies of women who smoke are more likely to have low birth weight, which in turn has been associated with other problems in motor, sensory, and cognitive areas.

Thalidomide causes a variety of severe malformations when taken during the early months of pregnancy. This example illustrates that drugs which are safe for animals are not necessarily safe for humans. It also shows that drugs can have negative effects with only isolated use. The thalidomide cases illustrate how the timing of exposure influences the effects of teratogens. They also show that teratogens are particularly dangerous during the embryonic period.

Narcotic drugs are carried in the blood of the woman and passed through the placenta to her embryo or fetus. Heroin users give birth to addicted children. Commonly, these children have suffered growth retardation in the uterus, and after birth they experience withdrawal. Since mothers who use narcotics often provide poor environments for their children, it is not clear whether prenatal exposure to the drug is the sole cause of the problems observed.

Cocaine increases the risk of low birthweight, still birth due to premature separation of the placenta, and a variety of congenital malformations.

Hormones are important in controlling prenatal development and for that reason they must be used with caution during pregnancy. For instance, DES is associated with high rates of genital-tract cancers in women and abnormalities of the testes in men.

Disease (pp. 119-120). Many viruses can pass through the placenta and affect the embryo or fetus. Pregnant women who have rubella early in pregnancy may give birth to children who are blind, deaf, or mentally retarded, and who may have heart defects. The effects of the disease depend on when it occurred during pregnancy. Different teratogens have similar effects when present at the same critical time in development. The same teratogen can have different effects depending upon the point in pregnancy at which exposure occurs.

Babies of women with Acquired Immune Deficiency Syndrome (AIDS) often show marked growth failure, with small heads and facial deformities. They acquire repeated infections, and their development is delayed.

Emotional Stress (p. 120). Research suggests a relationship between high levels of stress and difficulties during pregnancy. Mild periodic stress is of little concern.

Maternal Nutrition (pp. 120-121). Good nutrition before and during pregnancy is important for both mother and infant. Prenatal nutrition affects many aspects of development in the nervous system. Certain vitamins and minerals are needed during pregnancy. Both deficiencies and excesses of some vitamins can cause birth defects.

Maternal Age (pp. 121-122). Teenage mothers and women over 35 have higher rates of stillbirths and infant deaths. First pregnancies are more likely than others to end in miscarriage. After four pregnancies the probability of problems increases.

C. Detection and Treatment (pp. 122-123)

Many disorders can be detected early in pregnancy. Ultrasound can be used to diagnose structural anomolies. Amniocentesis can be used to diagnose a number of chromosomal anomolies. Amniocentesis can also detect neural tube defects such as absence of part of the brain or skull or failure of the spine to close. Chorionic villus sampling is a new technique that obtains cells from the placenta via a small tube passed through the vagina and cervix. These cells can be used to identify a wide range of genetic and chromosomal disorders.

D. Birth and Birth Complications (pp. 123-126)

The fetus gets ready for birth by moving into a head-down position. The mother's body responds with contractions, which help the fetus to go through the birth canal. Anoxia is a lengthy disruption in the infant's oxygen supply, which can result in damage to the baby's brain. Post-term babies may be too large to be delivered easily. They also may suffer from poor oxygenation because the placenta becomes less efficient as pregnancy goes beyond the expected duration. A standard set of medical tests and procedures is performed on the infant immediately and five minutes after birth in order to identify any problems that may have arisen from labor and delivery.

Low Birth Weight and Prematurity (p. 125). Babies who are born too small have increased risk of neurodevelopmental problems, congenital anomalies, and lung problems. Small birth size can be due to premature delivery, retarded growth and development in the uterus, or both. Low birth weight is associated with poverty and low maternal educational status.

Trends in Childbirth (pp. 125-126). There are many significant changes underway in childbirth practices in the United States. The Lamaze method and methods for natural childbirth are increasingly popular. There has also been an increase in deliveries by Caesarean section. Part of the increase is due to more accurate methods for detecting and monitoring problems the fetus may be encountering during labor and delivery.

IV. Prenatal Development in Context

(Pp. 126-128) Prenatal development occurs partly in a hereditary context: The genes include the blueprints for making a new person. Prenatal development also occurs in an environmental context involving hormones, nutrients, and other substances. Sometimes these substances come from the organism itself, sometimes they come from outside the womb via the placenta and the mother's bloodstream. The current environmental context is also an outcome of previous developmental changes. Genes alone do not provide all the information and support necessary for prenatal development. The infant's status at the end of prenatal development is modifiable , but it provides an important context for subsequent development.

SELF-TEST

Matching: Key Terms and Concepts

1.___polymorphism (p. 95)
2.___mutation (p. 95)
3.___gene (p. 95)
4.___gamete (p. 97)
5.___hormone (p. 101)
6.___phenotype (p. 103)
7.___conception (p. 104)
8.___blastocyst (p. 108)
9.___trophoblast (p. 108)
10.___organogenesis (p. 109)
11.___cephalocaudal (p. 112)
12.___proximodistal (p. 112)
13.___teratogen (p. 115)
14.___anoxia (p. 124)
15.___oxytocin (p. 124)

a. from the head downward
b. stimulates contractions
c. life-support system
d. rubella
e. beginning of development
f. segment of DNA
g. embryonic period
h. sperm or egg
i. glandular secretion
j. disruption of oxygen supply
k. naturally occurring changes in genes
l. observable physical trait
m. from center to extremities
o. variations on basic species patterns
n. structure of cells

Multiple Choice Questions

1. What is the process by which embryonic cells take on various forms and functions?

   a. prenatal development
   b. differentiation
   c. reorganization
   d. qualitative change
   (Objective 1, Conceptual)

2. Which process involves cells migrating, interacting with other cells, and building complex organs?

   a. differentation
   b. reorganization
   c. qualitative change
   d. germinal period
   (Objective 1, Factual)

3. The term gene refers to:

   a. the cell nucleus
   b. the reproductive cells
   c. chromosomes
   d. segments of DNA
   (Objective 2, Factual)

4. What is the term homologous used in reference to?

   a. chromosomes
   b. reproductive cells
   c. segments of DNA
   d. gametes
   (Objective 2, Conceptual)

5. Which of the following involves complete duplication of a cell's set of chromosomes?

   a. mitosis
   b. meiosis
   c. crossing over
   d. gamete production
   (Objective 3, Conceptual)

6. Which of the following refers to the process of producing sex cells with one half the full complement of chromosomes?

   a. mitosis
   b. fertilization
   c. meiosis
   d. crossing over

   (Objective 3, Factual)

7. Which of the following is illustrated by the effect of androgens on development of the male reproductice tract?

   a. genes
   b. the 23rd pair of chromosomes
   c. environmental context
   d. the Y chromosome

   (Objective 4, Conceptual)

8. Which of the following results in development of the female reproductive system during prenatal development?

   a. presence of androgens
   b. absence of androgens
   c. combination of androgens and estrogens
   d. presence of estrogens

   (Objective 4, Factual)

9. Suppose that the gene forms that determine eye color are Bl (blue), Bn (brown), and Gr (green). These would be:

   a. heterozygous
   b. homozygous
   c. phenotypes
   d. alleles

   (Objective 5, Conceptual)

10. Which of the following refers to observable characteristics?

    a. genotypes
    b. polygenic characteristics
    c. phenotypes
    d. modifiers

    (Objective 5, Factual)

11. When a sperm penetrates an ovum, the result is called a:

a. conception
b. genotype
c. zygote
d. homunculus
(Objective 6, Factual)

12. If two egg cells are released in the same cycle and fertilized, the result is:

a. monozygotic twins
b. dizygotic twins
c. genetically identical twins
d. ectopic pregnancy
(Objective 6, Factual)

13. The three major periods of prenatal development are, in order:

a. conception, embryonic, fetal
b. conception, germinal, embryonic
c. embryonic, fetal, germinal
d. germinal, embryonic, fetal
(Objective 7, Factual)

14. Organogenesis refers to the process in which all the vital organs and other major parts of the body form. This occurs during:

a. fetal period
b. conception
c. germinal period
d. embryonic period
(Objective 7, Factual)

15. Which of the following refers to an important type of interaction between cells in embryonic tissue?

a. embryonic inductions
b. embryonic organogesis
c. cephalocaudal patterns
d. proximodistal patterns
(Objective 7, Factual)

16. The heart and digestive system develop before limb buds, which develop before fingers and toes. What developmental principle does this illustrate?

a. cephalocaudal pattern
b. proximodistal pattern
c. reorganization
d. critical periods
(Objective 7, Conceptual)

17. Which of the following is the primary subject matter of teratology?

a. defects in the infant's genes
b. genetic disorders transmitted by parents' recessive alleles
c. environmental agents that can cause developmental defects prenatally
d. errors in meiosis that damage the chromosomes
(Objective 8, Conceptual)

18. Which of the following is most likely to cause serious prenatal effects?

a. mother contracting rubella early in pregnancy
b. thalidomide taken during the last two months of pregnancy
c. stress during pregnancy
d. having had two or three children previously
(Objective 8, Factual)

19. Both Down syndrome and neural tube defects can be detected by analyzing a sample of the fluid that surrounds the developing fetus. The technique used to withdraw the sample of fluid is:

a. ultrasound
b. amniocentesis
c. alpha-fetoprotein
d. chorionic villus sampling
(Objective 9, Conceptual)

20. Which of the following involves sampling cells from the developing placenta by a small tube passed through the vagina and cervix?

a. ultrasound
b. amniocentesis
c. alpha-fetoprotein
d. chorionic villus sampling
(Objective 9, Factual)

21. One of the complications of prolonged labor is reduced oxygen supply to the infant. This is refered to as:

a. breech birth
b. oxytocin
c. anoxia
d. Apgar condition 2
(Objective 10, Factual)

22. Which method of childbirth places special emphasis on psychological and behavioral ways of reducing fear and pain?

a. Leboyer
b. Caesarean section
c. Lamaze
d. all of the above
(Objective 10, Factual)

23. Which of the following childbirth methods focuses upon reducing the trauma of transition to extra-uterine life?

a. Leboyer
b. Caesarean section
c. Lamaze
d. regular hospital
(Objective 10, Conceptual)

24. Prenatal development unfolds within different contexts and their interactions. Which of the following factors is part of the prenatal contexts of development?

a. genes
b. hormones
c. nutrients and mother's body conditions
d. all of the above
(Objective 11, Factual)

ESSAY QUESTIONS

1. Much is still not known about genetic influences on development. It is clear, however, that genes alone cannot account for the events seen in normal prenatal development. What do genes require, aside from information encoded in DNA sequences, in order for prenatal development to occur?

2. Define the concept of a critical period during prenatal development and describe the effects of a teratogen that illustrates this concept.

ANSWER KEYS

Matching

1. o 2. k 3. f 4. h 5. i 6. l 7. e 8. n 9. c

10. g 11. a 12. m 13. d 14. j 15. b

Multiple Choice

1. b (p. 94)
2. b (p. 94)
3. d (p. 95)
4. a (p. 96)
5. a (p. 96)
6. c (p. 97)
7. c (p. 101)
8. b (p. 102)
9. d (p. 102)
10. c (p. 103)
11. c (p. 105)
12. b (p. 105)
13. d (p. 108)
14. d (p. 109)
15. a (p. 110)
16. b (p. 112)
17. c (p. 115)
18. a (p. 119)
19. b (pp. 122-123)
20. d (p. 123)
21. c (p. 124)
22. c (p. 125)
23. a (p. 126)
24. d (pp. 126-128)

Essay Questions

1. Genes require environmental support and input. This is provided by the environmental context in which genes always operate. This environmental context enables genes to be expressed and it also shapes developmental outcomes. The environment of genes is ultimately the cells of the body, which in turn are affected by a variety of outside factors from nutrients to drugs and viruses that enter the organism's bloodstream. The genetic environment is also influenced by the organism's own developmental history. Therefore, it is best to think of genes as only one part of an intricate developmental system that includes heredity and environment **(p. 100).**

2. A critical period is a limited time during which some part of the developing organism is especially susceptible to a particular environmental influence. That structures are more susceptible to damage at different times is illustrated by the fact that particular effects of drugs like thalidomide are linked to exposure at specific points in pregnancy. In fact, thalidomide has few negative effects if it is taken beyond the eighth week. At this point, the beginnings of the major body parts are already formed, and they are less susceptible to disruption than they would have been when they were just becoming organized **(pp. 112, 117-118).**

Chapter 5
First Adaptations

LEARNING OBJECTIVES

When you have studied the material in this chapter, you will be able to:

1. Name four built-in capacities that help newborn infants adapt.
2. Distinguish among several states of infant sleep and wakefulness.
3. Define the term reflex and give examples of the different classes of reflexes.
4. Describe the sensory capabilities of infants in the realms of vision, hearing, smell, and taste.
5. Define the term perception and describe the development of infant visual perceptual abilities.
6. Describe key principles and patterns in motor development, and describe the emergence of controlled eye movements, reaching and grasping, and walking.
7. Explain habituation and give an example.
8. Describe associative learning and explain and give examples of two types of associative learning.
9. Explain imitative learning and give an example.
10. Explain the concept of preparedness and give an example.

CHAPTER SUMMARY

(Pp. 139-141) Infants are equipped with a set of built-in capacities that help them adapt to the world. These include reflexes, perceptual abilities, motor skills, and learning abilities. Infants are surprisingly well equipped and competent. Infants' competencies often meet a direct survival need. Their competencies arise from both the content and the organization of their behavior. Infants respond selectively to the environment. And they can detect relationships between actions and their consequences. These connections are called contingencies.

I. Infant States

(Pp. 141-143) Infant states and transitions between them are important to consider because infants respond very differently to the environment depending on their current state. Infant states are classified as: quiet sleep, active sleep, awake and quiet, awake and active, fussing, and crying.

Newborns spend more than sixteen hours sleeping each day. The pattern of sleep also changes. Active and quiet sleep are irregularly intermixed in infants. Sleep patterns in infancy are related to progress in neural development.

Three different types of crying have been reported: hungry cries, upset cries, and pain cries. Sucking has a strong soothing effect on most infants.

II. Reflexes in the Newborn

(Pp. 143-144) A reflex is an automatic or built-in reaction elicited by particular stimuli. Reflexes provide basic forms of organized, adaptive response to the environment before the infant has had the opportunity to learn. Many early reflexes are modified by experience and thus serve as the basis for rapid acquisition of new behaviors.

A. Survival Reflexes **(pp. 144-145)**

Sucking and several other reflexes that are present at birth serve important survival functions. Some of these reflexes remain stable throughout life and some others disappear as the infant acquires more skills.

B. Other Reflexes **(pp. 145-146)**

Some reflexes seen at birth have no apparent survival value and disappear with age. But the basic behavior patterns shown in these reflexes later become part of more sophisticated voluntary actions. The grasping reflex and the stepping reflex are examples of this kind of reflex.

III. Sensing and Perceiving the World

A. Sensory Systems in the Newborn **(pp. 146-152)**

Vision **(pp. 146-149).** Acuity refers to the fineness of detail a person can see. Babies have problems discerning the fine details of objects. Recent studies show that infants' eyes do focus in response to the distance of an object.

Infants as young as two months have a degree of sensitivity to color. Color vision may reach adult levels by 3 to 4 months of age.

Hearing **(pp. 149-151).** Loud noises will elicit movements from a fetus at 31 weeks. Hearing sensitivity in newborns can be determined by monitoring eye blinks, changes in heart rate, and changes in the brain's electrical activity as sounds are presented. By 5 to 8 months of age, infants are very good at detecting changes in pitch. They are sensitive to a broad range of pitches and hear higher frequencies than adults do.

Although speech perception changes with age and depends partly on experience, the basic sensory system required to learn language seems to be genetically given.

Smell and Taste **(pp. 151-152).** Infants' and adults' reactions to various odors are quite similar. Infants can discriminate sweet tastes from others, but it is not clear whether they can discriminate among bitter, sour, and salty tastes.

B. The Organization of Infant Sensory Behavior **(p. 152)**

The young infant uses its great array of sensory capacities in an organized way. Infants' processing of their environments seems to be guided by certain rules.

C. Development of Perceptual Abilities **(pp. 152-157)**

Perception refers to the process by which the brain interprets information from the senses, giving it order and meaning.

Depth and Distance Perception (pp. 153-156). Research by Gibson and Walk suggests that infants can perceive depth by 6 or 7 months of age. Campos has shown that 2-months-old babies can distinguish different depths.

Some information about how far away objects are arises from the fact that visual information reaches the brain from two eyes. These are called binocular depth cues. Aslin has found that by one month of age, babies converge their eyes when looking at nearby objects and let their eyes diverge when looking at distant objects. By 5 months of age, infants use convergence as an effective cue to determining distance when they reach for something.

Depth cues are also available through each eye independently, as when one object hides part of another object that is behind it (interposition). These are called monocular depth cues. Infants begin to use interposition at the same age they start using linear perspective. This suggests that neural maturation plays a role in determining the timing of these changes.

Size and Shape Constancy (pp. 156-157). The size and shape of images on the retina changes if distance, location, or head position changes. And yet we see objects as having constant size and shape. These important perceptual processes are called size constancy and shape constancy. Shape constancy emerges at around 3 months of age. These processes are obviously critical to identifying particular people and telling them apart.

Perception of Faces (p. 156). In order to recognize faces, an infant must distinguish one face from another, and yet treat the same face as the same, even when it is in different positions or expressions. Infants can recognize pictures of their mother by the age of 3 months. By 5 months infants remember and distinguish among the faces of strangers.

IV. Infant Motor Skills

(Pp. 158-159) The developmental principle of differentiation is particularly evident in motor development. At first, movements are global and poorly defined. Eventually they develop into a set of precise skills adapted to specific functions. The cephalocaudal pattern refers to the tendency for control over motor movements to progress from head to toe. The proximodistal pattern refers to the tendency for control over motor movements to progress from the center of the body to the extremities.

A. Eye Movements (pp. 159-160)

Infants and adults move their eyes from one object to another in rapid jerks called saccadic eye movements. Once on an object, the eyes follow it with smooth pursuit eye movements. Infants can track slowly moving objects with saccadic and smooth pursuit eye movements by age 2 months. By 4 months they can track rapidly moving objects.

B. Reaching and Grasping **(p. 161)**

Early in infancy, reaching and grasping are reflexes rather than voluntary actions. As voluntary reaching and grasping begin to appear, the early reflexive responses gradually disappear.

C. Walking **(pp. 161-163)**

The onset of walking depends both on maturation of the muscles and nervous system and on practice. Some studies seem to indicate that maturation plays a greater role in the onset of walking than does a child's practice. But the onset of walking can be speeded up with enough appropriate practice.

V. Infant Learning

A. Habituation **(pp. 164-165)**

An infant's attention to a stimulus decreases if it is presented again and again in a short period of time. This is called habituation. It is one of the first signs that newborns retain information about their environments.

B. Associative Learning **(pp. 165-168)**

Classical Conditioning **(pp. 165-167)**. Classical conditioning is a learning process in which a new stimulus becomes capable of eliciting an established reflex response. Extinction refers to the gradual decline of the conditioned response. Recent studies have appeared to demonstrate that infants can learn by classical conditioning, although some such studies are criticized for not ruling out alternative explanations. Classical conditioning by itself cannot explain the appearance of new behaviors, since the response to be conditioned must be one the person already performs.

Instrumental Conditioning **(pp. 167-168)**. As early as three days after birth, the frequency with which an infant performs a behavior can be influenced by the consequences of the behavior. Positive and negative reinforcement increase the probability of a particular behavior. Punishment, the presentation of a negative stimulus following a behavior, decreases the probability of such a behavior. Instrumental conditioning is also called operant learning. It is one means of acquiring new behaviors. The ease of instrumental conditioning in babies suggests that infants come preadapted to respond to contingencies.

C. Imitative Learning **(pp. 168-170)**

Imitation is a rapid and powerful mechanism for learning. Imitation can only occur when the infant becomes able to (1) map what is seen into a set of movements of their own and (2) form some memory of these movements for future use. Piaget argued that these abilities develop gradually during the first two years. Uzgiris outlines four steps in the development of imitation.

D. The Concept of Preparedness **(pp. 170-171)**

An infant's ability to learn depends very much on what is to be learned and how. The term preparedness refers to the fact that biological biases in the infant's learning abilities seem to make some things easier to learn than others.

VI. The Preadapted Infant

(Pp. 171-172) Infants are biased or preadapted to select and attend to certain types of features. They are attracted to human voices and tend to follow horizontal movements of the caregiver's face. They are also preadapted to detect contingencies. These are important foundations for adaptation to life after birth.

SELF-TEST

Matching: Key Terms and Concepts

1.___contingency (p. 141)

2.___neonate (p. 141)

3.___infant state (p. 141)

4.___reflex (p. 143)

5.___acuity (p. 146)

6.___saccade (p. 146)

7.___binocular depth cue (p. 154)

8.___monocular depth cue (p. 155)

9.___pursuit eye movements (p. 160)

10.___orienting response (p. 164)

11.___pairing UCS and CS (p. 165)

12.___behavior-reinforcement (p. 167)

13.___shaping (p. 167)

14.___imitative learning (p. 168)

15.___preparedness (p. 170)

a. operant conditioning

b. interposition

c. mimicking other's behavior

d. sleep

e. classical conditioning

f. newborn

g. link between act and consequence

h. automatic built-in reaction

i. genetic predisposition in learning

j. convergence

k. jerky eye movements

l. continuous smooth eye motions

m. fineness of visual detail

n. attending to a new stimulus

o. gradual approximation to a target behavior

Multiple Choice Questions

1. Which of the following are included in the newborn's built-in adaptive capabilities?

    a. reflexes, states, and motor skills
    b. reflexes, states, motor skills, and learning abilities
    c. reflexes, motor skills, and perceptual and learning abilities
    d. all of the above
    (Objective 1, Factual)

2. That infants are interested in human voices illustrates the fact that:

    a. infants detect relationships between actions and their effects
    b. infants selectively respond to their environment
    c. infants' competencies involve organization of behavior
    d. infants' competencies often meet survival needs
    (Objective 1, Conceptual)

3. Which of the following is the basic rest-activity cycle of infants?

    a. sleeping and wakefulness
    b. sleeping and crying
    c. wakefulness and crying
    d. sleeping, wakefulness, and crying
    (Objective 2, Conceptual)

4. Research on the crying state has shown that:

    a. there are three patterns: hungry cries, upset cries, and pain cries
    b. there are two patterns: fussing and crying
    c. crying occupies the least amount of time of the infant's states
    d. all of the above
    (Objective 2, Factual)

5. Mary strokes her infant's cheek and the baby responds by turning the head toward the side that was touched and opening its mouth to suck. What is this early reflex called?

    a. Moro reflex
    b. tonic neck reflex
    c. rooting reflex
    d. sucking reflex
    (Objective 3, Conceptual)

6. The grasping and stepping reflexes are examples of reflexes that:

   a. have survival function
   b. remain stable throughout a person's life
   c. disappear as the infant grows older
   d. become voluntary actions later in life
   (Objective 3, Factual)

7. Which of the following is a visual reflex that helps to determine the degree of detail the infant sees?

   a. acuity
   b. saccade
   c. accommodation
   d. motivation to look at things
   (Objective 4, Conceptual)

8. At 2 weeks of age, the child sees at 20 feet what an adult with normal vision can see at 300 feet. Five months later, the infant sees at 20 feet what an adult can see at 100 feet. This illustrates the improvement in visual ___________.

   a. acuity
   b. saccade
   c. regard
   d. motivation to look at things
   (Objective 4, Conceptual)

9. Research on hearing indicates that:

   a. infants are good at discriminating among various speech sounds
   b. speech perception changes with development and experience
   c. the sensory basis for language learning is present at birth
   d. all of the above
   (Objective 4, Factual)

10. Which of the following tastes can infants most surely discriminate?
    a. sweet
    b. sour
    c. bitter
    d. salty
    (Objective 4, Factual)

11. The process by which the brain interprets information from the senses, giving it order and meaning, is:

a. sensation
b. organization of infant sensory behavior
c. perception
d. all of the above
(Objective 5, Conceptual)

12. The visual cliff is a device used by Gibson and Walk to study:

a. binocular and monocular depth cues
b. depth perception
c. size and shape constancy
d. perception of faces
(Objective 5, Factual)

13. Which of the following are binocular depth cues?

a. linear perspective and interposition
b. interposition and convergence
c. convergence and retinal disparity
d. retinal disparity and linear perspective
(Objective 5, Conceptual)

14. What is the term for the depth cue that involves convergence of parallel lines as they extend away from the viewer?

a. convergence
b. linear perspective
c. retinal disparity
d. interposition
(Objective 5, Conceptual)

15. Which of the following is illustrated by the refinement of infant movements from global to a set of precise movements adapted to specific functions?

a. cephalocaudal pattern of development
b. proximodistal pattern of development
c. development of walking
d. differentiation principle of development
(Objective 6, Conceptual)

16. Which of the following is illustrated by the fact that refined eye movements and sucking develop before reaching and grasping?

    a. differentiation principle of development
    b. proximodistal pattern of development
    c. cephalocaudal pattern of development
    d. none of the above

    (Objective 6, Conceptual)

17. Research has demonstrated that the onset of walking depends on

    a. the maturation of the nervous system
    b. maturation of the muscles and practice
    c. practice
    d. all of the above

    (Objective 6, Factual)

18. An infant is presented with a blue and red square that captures his attention. After 30 seconds of looking at the square, the infant loses interest in it. Which of the following learning processes explains this?

    a. habituation
    b. orienting response
    c. associative learning
    d. conditioning

    (Objective 7, Conceptual)

19. Which of the following occurs when an infant becomes very quiet and stares into its mother's face in response to a new sound the mother makes?

    a. habituation
    b. orienting response
    c. classical conditioning
    d. operant conditioning

    (Objective 7, Conceptual)

20. Elizabeth takes a glass in the living room and it breaks when it drops on the floor. Her father tells her not to do it again and sends Elizabeth to her room. This is an example of

    a. positive reinforcement
    b. negative reinforcement
    c. shaping
    d. punishment

    (Objective 8, Conceptual)

21. Which of the following increases the rate at which a behavior occurs?

    a. negative reinforcement
    b. punishment
    c. shaping
    d. none of the above

    (Objective 8, Factual)

22. Which of the following is the first step in Uzgiris's summary of the stages through which imitation develops?

    a. matching others' behaviors by similarity of perceptual consequences
    b. reproducing behaviors without monitoring success
    c. imitating behaviors that the child has never performed before
    d. imitating unfamiliar behaviors and monitoring accuracy

    (Objective 9, Factual)

23. Which of the following mechanisms allows an infant to learn the most new behavior in the shortest time?

    a. habituation
    b. classical conditioning
    c. operant conditioning
    d. imitative learning

    (Objective 9, Factual)

24. Which of the following is illustrated by the fact that young babies so readily smile, detect contingencies, and orient to faces and voices?

    a. the role of experience in learning
    b. that the infant is preadapted
    c. the role of operant conditioning
    d. all of the above

    (Objective 9, Conceptual)

ESSAY QUESTIONS

1. Why has infant state been the subject of so much research?

2. Summarize Uzgiris's four-step model of the development of imitation, and explain why imitation is so important for learning.

ANSWER KEYS

Matching

1. g 2. f 3. d 4. h 5. m 6. k 7. j 8. b 9. l 10. n

11. e 12. a 13. o 14. c 15. i

Multiple Choice

1. c (p. 140)	13. c (p. 153)
2. b (p. 140)	14. b (p. 155)
3. d (p. 141)	15. d (p. 158)
4. a (p. 142)	16. c (p. 159)
5. c (p. 145)	17. d (p. 162)
6. c (p. 145)	18. a (p. 164)
7. b (p. 146)	19. b (p. 164)
8. a (p. 147)	20. d (p. 167)
9. d (p. 151)	21. a (p. 167)
10. a (p. 151)	22. a (p. 168)
11. c (p. 153)	23. d (p. 168)
12. b (p. 153)	24. b (p. 171)

Essay Questions

1. Infant state has been studied in great detail for several reasons. First, it is an example of organization in the infant's behavior. States are not random. Second, state and state changes can be used to monitor underlying changes in neural organization. State is also important because the infant's learning is significantly affected by its state. Finally, state has been studied because it has an important impact on the infant's social environment. Infants who have unpredictable states, are difficult to rouse to alertness, or are often in distressed states are difficult for adults to interact with and handle well **(pp. 141-143).**

2. Step 1. During the first six months of life infants can match behaviors of others or reproduce their own behaviors based on similarity of perceptual consequences.

   Step 2. At 6 to 12 months of age, babies try to imitate behaviors they see or hear that they have never done before. They often fail altogether or only manage an incomplete copy of the target behavior.

   Step 3. At 12 to 18 months of age, babies are much better at imitating unfamiliar behaviors. Their imitations are frequently accompanied by checking of the other person's behavior to assure that the imitation is accurate.

   Step 4. Beginning around 18 months, children's imitations, even of novel behaviors, become very accurate and require little checking to monitor success. They become highly skilled at imitating actions, even when they cannot directly monitor the success of their own imitations.

   Imitation is an important form of learning because it allows the infant to learn complex new behaviors in much less time than would be required by shaping. In addition, imitation does not require a partner to time contingencies or deliver reinforcers or punishment **(pp. 168-169).**

Chapter 6
Infant Cognitive Development

LEARNING OBJECTIVES

When you have studied the material in this chapter, you will be able to:

1. Describe Piaget's sensorimotor stage of cognitive development and its six substages.
2. Define primary, secondary, and tertiary circular reactions and explain the role of goal-directed chains of behavior in cognitive development.
3. Define object permanence and describe its development in each of the six sensorimotor substages.
4. Summarize the difficulties involved in explaining how and why cognitive development advances from one stage to the next.
5. Describe the course of memory development in the sensorimotor period.
6. Define the Piagetian concepts adaptation, assimilation, accommodation, equilibration, schemes, and reflective abstraction.
7. Describe reformulations of and alternatives to Piaget's theories suggested by Kurt Fischer, Robbie Case, and Jerome Bruner. Summarize the main criticisms leveled at Piaget's theory.
8. Define executive processing space and mastery play.
9. Describe the constraints on cognitive functioning that are characteristic of infancy.
10. Identify the three general themes of cognitive development in the first two years of life.

CHAPTER SUMMARY

(Pp. 175-177) There are three general themes in the development of cognitive abilities in infancy. Cognitive development is orderly. Infants are active participants in their own cognitive development. And there are both advances and continued limitations in the infants' cognitive abilities. Key achievements in infancy include understanding of causality, means and ends relationships, and object permanence.

I. The Course of Infant Cognitive Development

(Pp. 178-179) The first theorist to study cognitive development was Jean Piaget. He described cognitive development in infancy as the sensorimotor period. Most develop mental psychologists are now agreed on the abilities the infant acquires in the first two years.

The sensorimotor period is divided into six distinctive stages that all infant's progress through in the same order.

Stage 1: Reflexes (Birth to 1 month) **(p. 179).** The first stage of the sensorimotor period involves the infant's refinement of genetically programmed reflexes. This stage is also referred to as Level 0 in Kurt Fischer's theory of cognitive development and as Substage 0: Operational Consolidation in Robbie Case's theory of cognitive development.

Stage 2: Simple Actions (1-4 months) **(pp. 179-180).** Primary circular reactions are behaviors produced by the infant's movement of its body and repeated in order to produce an interesting sensory outcome. The starting point for a primary circular reaction is accidental rather than intentional behavior. Fischer terms this stage Simple Actions. Case combines Stages 1 and 2 into the period of Operational Consolidation.

Stage 3: Actions on Objects (4-8 months) **(pp. 181-182).** Secondary circular reactions differ from behavior of earlier stages in being directed toward external objects. The infant actively investigates the effects of its behavior on objects in the environment.

Stage 4: Coordination of Action (8-12 months) **(pp. 182-183).** This stage if characterized by the first use of goal-directed chains of behavior. Piaget called this "the coordination of secondary schemes." This stage marks the first emergence of purposeful behavior, for example, the infant's moving a dog out of its path to reach an electrical outlet. Infants will also begin to imitate simple infrequent behaviors they observe others displaying.

Stage 5: Exploration by Variations of Actions (12-18 months) **(pp. 183-184).** Tertiary (third order) reactions are similar to primary and secondary reactions. The original event occurs by accident and is interesting, and the infant attempts to repeat it. The key difference is that now the infant begins to intentionally vary the behaviors that produced the interesting event. This type of trial and error exploration leads the child to understand cause and effect relationships. Case describes this as the period of Elaborated Coordination. Fischer defines it in terms of Systems of Actions. This is the last stage of infant cognitive development in Case's theory.

Stage 6: Beginnings of Representational Thought **(18-24 months) (pp. 184-185).** Piaget, Case, and Fischer view this stage as the transition from sensorimotor development to the use of mental representations of the world. Fischer calls this stage Simple Representations. Deferred imitation, the ability to let one object stand for something else, and problem solving through mental representations rather than sensorimotor schemes are key accomplishments here.

II. Developing the Concept of Objects

(P. 185) Object permanence is the understanding that objects continue to exist even though the object can no longer be seen. This understanding is acquired gradually during the sensorimotor period.

A. Development Through the Six Sensorimotor Stages (pp. 185-188)

Stages 1 and 2 **(pp. 185-186).** No object permanence concept. Infants will track nearby objects visually. If the object is even partially covered, the infant will behave as if the object has disappeared.

Stage 3 **(pp. 186-187).** The infant will reach for partially covered objects but does not understand the continued existence of completely covered objects.

Stage 4 **(p. 187).** The infant will search for hidden objects. If the object is not found in the first place the infant searches, the infant behaves as if the object no longer exists.

Stage 5 **(p. 187).** The infant will look in more than one location for the missing object, but does not understand that the object can be moved when it is out of sight. Assumes it must be near where it disappeared.

Stage 6 **(pp. 187-188).** Complete concept of object permanence. Understands that an object continues to exist even when it is out of sight or out of sight and moved after disappearing.

B. Continuing Research on Infant's Understanding of Objects **(pp. 188-189)**

Researchers generally agree on the sequence of steps in acquiring object permanence but disagree as to the timing of the steps. The age associated with acquiring a given level of object permanence seems to depend upon the criteria used to score success in object permanence tasks. Piaget's criteria may have reflected limitations of infant's memory more than its ability to understand the principles of object permanence.

III. Memory Development During Infancy

A. Memory in the First Six Months of Life **(pp. 190-192)**

Rudimentary memory abilities are clearly present in early infancy. Habituation studies demonstrate that infants recognize familiar events. Infants from 2 to 4 months old can remember events up to 14 days. Infants younger than 4 months can remember only single features of pictures. Older infants can remember the relationship among simple features of a picture.

B. Memory in the Second Half-Year **(pp. 192-195)**

At this point infants have long-term memories. They respond differently to mother and father and also begin to use words, which suggests the presence of long-term memory. By 7 months, infants are able to form general, broad categories (for example, female faces and male faces). In addition, early rudimentary processing of numerical information into long-term memory begins. This is called the perception of numerosity.

IV. Explanations of Cognitive Development

A. Piaget's Theory **(p. 195)**

Piaget's theory was the first comprehensive theory of cognitive development. He proposed that cognitive development advances by the child's active construction of a system that enables him or her to understand the world. This ongoing construction enables the child to progress through the sensorimotor period, concrete operations, and finally formal operations.

<u>The General Nature of Development</u> **(pp. 195-197).** An infant acquires knowledge through motor acts and perceptual awareness. Interaction between motor acts and perceptual awareness allows cognitive growth. The infant is both active in actual motor movements and active in constructing an understanding of the world. Limitations characteristic of this age are generally due to the infant's restricted abilities in interacting with the environment. Although most theorists agree with Piaget about the infant's limitations, Case and Fischer do not agree with Piaget's view that general logical structures limit understanding at each level of development.

Processes of Change (pp. 197-200). Piaget explained all developmental change in terms of two processes, adaptation and equilibration. Adaptation is the process by which a person changes behavior or underlying thinking in order to function more effectively in a certain situation. There are two subprocesses of adaptation: assimilation and accommodation. Assimilation is the process of applying an existing capability to various situations. Accommodation is the process of making modifications of the existing capabilities in order to continue dealing successfully with the world. Adaptation is the result of assimilation and accommodation working together. Schemes are mental structures that underlie and organize patterns of behavior. The schemes acquired in the sensorimotor period are very important because they are the foundation for the acquisition of skills in later development.

B. Alternatives to Piaget's Theory (pp. 200-205)

Reassessing the Concept of Stages (pp. 200-201). Piaget has been criticized for his use of a stage model of cognitive development. Different infants clearly acquire the same skill at different ages. In addition, the same infant may acquire related skills at different ages. Piaget used the term decalage when referring to unevenness in different areas of development.

Cognitive Constraints in Infancy: Fischer and Case (pp. 201-204). Baldwin emphasized limited attention span as an important cognitive constraint on infant cognitive development. Pascual-Leone discussed constraints related to mental power. Fischer and Case refer to cognitive constraints in infancy in terms of working memory. The amount of information that can be held in working memory increases with age. Case refers to working memory as executive processing space. In Case's view, maturation and experiential factors influence the efficiency rather than the capacity of executive processing space.

The Approach of Jerome Bruner (pp. 204-205). Bruner describes cognitive development in terms of changes in modes of representation. The enactive mode corresponds to Piaget's sensorimotor period. Like Piaget, Bruner emphasizes the role of motor activity in infant cognitive development. In addition, Bruner agrees that infants are active and intrinsically motivated to interact with the environment. Bruner calls this mastery play. Bruner has been willing to attribute goals and intentions to infants at a much earlier age than Piaget.

V. Advances and Limitations: An Overview

Infants begin with a finite set of inborn responses and gradually acquire more complex and purposeful behaviors. Infants are busy, active learners and actively master their environment. Through the use of adaptation, the infant becomes more effective in dealing with environmental demands. Although the infant makes great strides in cognitive development, it still has a distinctive set of limitations at the end of the sensorimotor period.

SELF-TEST

Matching: Key Terms and Concepts

1. ___adaptation (p. 197)
2. ___secondary circular reactions (p. 181)
3. ___reflex (p. 179)
4. ___schemes (p. 199)
5. ___working memory (p. 201)
6. ___primary circular reactions (p. 179)
7. ___bifocal coordination (p. 182)
8. ___tertiary circular reactions (p. 183)
9. ___mental power (p. 201)
10. ___equilibration (p. 198)
11. ___reflective abstraction (p. 199)
12. ___mastery play (p. 204)
13. ___mechanisms of development (p. 197)
14. ___deferred imitation (p. 184)
15. ___enactive mode (p. 204)

a. simple actions

b. explorations by variations of actions

c. provides feedback to help the infant acquire skills

d. sign of representational thought

e. actions on objects

f. leads to more effective adaptations

g. adaptation and equilibration

h. assimilation and accommodation

i. acquisition of more complex abilities in thinking

j. Jerome Bruner

k. a cognitive constraint

l. limited attention span

m. built-in pattern of behavior

n. goal-directed chains of behavior

o. operations

Multiple Choice Questions

1. Which of the following is not considered one of the major achievements of infant cognitive development?

   a. understanding of causality
   b. object permanence
   c. understanding of means and ends relationships
   d. all of the above
   (Objective 1, Factual)

2. Which developmental psychologist describes the first stage of cognitive development as the sensorimotor period?

   a. Robbie Case
   b. Jerome Bruner
   c. Jean Piaget
   d. Kurt Fischer
   (Objective 1, Factual)

3. General thinking skills common to all normal infants are referred to as:

   a. intelligence
   b. cognitive development
   c. cognitive abilities
   d. sensorimotor schemes
   (Objective 1, Factual)

4. Which of the following is an example of an infant <u>reflex</u>?

   a. watching a fast-moving object
   b. sucking fingers during sleep
   c. shaking a rattle in a new way
   d. kicking a toy to emit a sound
   (Objective 1, Conceptual)

5. Primary circular reactions are:

a. repetition of an accidentally produced body movement
b. actions on objects that produce interesting events
c. goal-directed chains of behavior
d. trial and error variations in play with an object
(Objective 2, Factual)

6. Bifocal coordination is also known as:

a. elaborated coordination
b. coordination of schemes
c. operational coordination
d. relations of actions
(Objective 2, Factual)

7. Deferred imitation signifies the beginning of:

a. representational thought
b. circular reactions
c. object permanence
d. the perception of numerosity
(Objective 2, Factual)

8. An infant is observed moving a stuffed animal out of its way to reach an electrical outlet. This is an example of:

a. a primary circular reaction
b. coordination of secondary schemes
c. a secondary circular reaction
d. decalage
(Objective 2, Conceptual)

9. Dropping a variety of toys down stairs one by one is an example of:

a. a secondary circular reaction
b. a tertiary circular reaction
c. a primary circular reaction
d. a goal directed chain of behavior
(Objective 2, Conceptual)

10. An infant repeatedly hits a ball on the side of its crib and squeals in delight. This is an example of:

a. object permanence
b. a tertiary circular reaction
c. a primary circular reaction
d. a secondary circular reaction
(Objective 2, Conceptual)

11. The ability to understand that a toy exists even though it can not be seen is known as:

a. accommodation
b. decalage
c. reflective abstraction
d. object permanence
(Objective 3, Factual)

12. At what age did Piaget place the emergence of the object permanence concept?

a. 0-1 month
b. 1-4 months
c. 8-12 months
d. 12-18 months
(Objective 3, Factual)

13. Habituation studies with young infants provide important evidence about:

a. alertness to changes in the environment
b. performance on simple visual tasks
c. early visual acuity
d. early memory capabilities
(Objective 5, Factual)

14. Schemes are also known as:

a. equilibration
b. mastery play
c. operations
d. deferred imitation
(Objective 6, Factual)

15. Which of the following terms refers to mental structures that underlie and organize patterns of behavior?

a. schemes
b. circular reactions
c. cognitive abilities
d. modes of representation
(Objective 6, Factual)

16. The two key mechanisms of development in Piaget's theory are:

a. adaptation and equilibration
b. assimilation and accommodation
c. schemes and operations
d. working memory and executive processing space
(Objective 6, Factual)

17. Assimilation involves:

a. mastery play
b. applying available schemes
c. deferred imitation
d. modifying reflexes
(Objective 6, Factual)

18. When an infant puts a block in its mouth, adaptation involves:

a. assimilation
b. accommodation
c. equilibration
d. mastery play
(Objective 6, Conceptual)

19. Jerome Bruner refers to the sensorimotor period of cognitive development in terms of:

a. systems of actions
b. the enactive mode
c. relations of actions
d. single representations
(Objective 7, Factual)

20. Maturation and experiential factors both influence the efficiency of:

a. reflective abstraction
b. representational thought
c. goal-directed chains of behavior
d. executive processing space
(Objective 7, Factual)

21. What concept did Piaget use to explain the fact that infants of the same age may be in different stages of cognitive development?

a. adaptation
b. equilibration
c. reflective abstraction
d. decalage
(Objective 7, Conceptual)

22. All of the following terms imply cognitive constraint except one. Which does not imply a cognitive constraint?

a. working memory
b. executive processing space
c. schemes
d. mental power
(Objective 8, Factual)

23. Which of the following is a major constraint on cognitive abilities in Case's view of infant development?

a. attention span
b. available schemes
c. recognition memory
d. executive processing space
(Objective 9, Factual)

24. Which of the following is not a general theme in infant cognitive development?

a. infants are active participants
b. cognitive development is orderly in nature
c. there are both advances and continued limitations in infancy
d. infants are under the control of environmental stimuli
(Objective 10, Factual)

ESSAY QUESTIONS

1. Describe the course of memory development in infancy.

2. Briefly summarize two recent criticisms related to Piaget's theory of cognitive development.

VIGNETTE HIGHLIGHT

Multiple Choice Questions

1. Malcolm is observed lying on his back with his arms cycling around and around and his feet kicking vigorously. This is an example of:

   a. a primary circular reaction
   b. a circular reaction
   c. a secondary circular reaction
   d. a tertiary circular reaction

2. Malcolm is observed bringing a fist up to his mouth and sucking on all five fingers instantly. This is an example of:

   a. a primary circular reaction
   b. a circular reaction
   c. a secondary circular reaction
   d. a tertiary circular reaction

3. Mikey is observed throwing his toys, one by one, over the side of his crib. This is an example of:

   a. a primary circular reaction
   b. a circular reaction
   c. a secondary circular reaction
   d. a tertiary circular reaction

4. Meryl is observed looking very serious while stacking brightly colored rings on a plastic post. What is the most likely reason for her serious expression?

   a. her characteristically grouchy temperament
   b. her mother's mood
   c. the attention and effort required to stack the rings
   d. representational thought

Essay Questions

Mikey is a healthy, active baby. His parents are experiencing some stress in their marriage. In fact, one of the reasons for having another baby was to bring Christine and Frank Gordon (the parents) closer. The financial situation is strained and Christine has begun to work part time out of the home. Her husband is not enthusiastic about her working. Mikey doesn't seem to be having the intended effect on their marriage.

1. Explain how this situation might have a negative influence on Mikey's cognitive development.

2. Suggest two family or environmental factors that could prevent the a family situation like the Gordons' from having negative effects on the infant's cognitive development. Explain why they would help.

ANSWER KEYS

Matching

1. h   2. e   3. m   4. o   5. k   6. a   7. n   8. b   9. l

10. f   11. i   12. c   13. g   14. d   15. j

Multiple Choice

1. d (p. 177)	13. d (p. 190)
2. c (p. 178)	14. c (pp. 199-200)
3. c (p. 176)	15. a (p. 199)
4. b (p. 179)	16. a (p. 197-198)
5. a (pp. 179-180)	17. b (p. 198)
6. b (p. 182)	18. a (p. 198)
7. a (pp. 184-185)	19. b (p. 204)
8. b (p. 182)	20. d (p. 202)
9. b (p. 183)	21. d (p. 200)
10. d (pp. 181-182)	22. c (pp. 201-202)
11. d (p. 185)	23. d (p. 202)
12. c (p. 206)	24. d (pp. 176-177)

Essay Questions

1. During the first few months of life, infants habituate to familiar sights and sounds. This suggests that there is enough memory to recognize familiar events. Infants of only a few weeks can remember simple types of stimuli over a 24-hour period. Infants from 2 to 4 months can remember events up to 14 days. In addition, 5-month-old infants can remember faces for up to two weeks. In general, studies show that infants younger than 4 months can remember only single features of pictures, while infants older than 4 months can remember the relationship among simple features of a picture.

   In the second half of the first year, infants have long-term memory. They respond differently to mother and father and also begin to use words. By 7 months, infants are able to form general, broad categories, such as female faces (pp. 185-188).

2. Problems in assessing object permanence. Studies suggest that if the infant does not have to actively search for a hidden object, as proof of object permanence, it may exist as early as 5 to 8 months of age. In fact, it seems that the criteria that Piaget used to evaluate the presence of object permanence reflect the limitations of infants' memory more than the ability to understand the principles of object permanence (pp. 188-189).

   Problems with using a stage model of development. Many researchers have shown inconsistencies across infants in regard to when a particular skill is acquired. Some infants develop a skill sooner than others or do not attain all the skills of a particular stage in the sequence that Piaget proposed. This unevenness of development has led theorists such as Case and Fischer to suggest alternative explanations of cognitive development. Their models emphasize continuous rather than stagelike change.

VIGNETTE ANSWER KEYS

Multiple Choice

1. b (p. 179) 2. a (p. 179) 3. d (p. 183) 4. c (p. 182)

Essay Questions

1. Financial problems and the need for both parents to work can have negative effects on the physical environment in the home and on the parents' energy level and mood when Mikey needs care or wants to play. If there is not enough room in the house to allow Mikey much floor freedom, he is likely to spend extra time in a playpen or in just one room. This could limit his opportunities to learn new sensorimotor schemes. It also limits the number of challenges he can face and overcome.

   The marital problems can also have a negative effect on Mikey's cognitive development. Parents are less able to watch, support, and get involved in an infant's play if they have personal problems on their mind. Parental support and involvement in an infant's play can enrich it in many ways. An alert adult can "arrange" for interesting things to happen, or help a child have a success at something that is just a bit beyond his or her sensorimotor level. Marital problems can be exhausting, and this can take away from the quality of parent-infant play.

2. More living space would clearly help. The crowding in the Gordon's first home probably limited how much exploration Mikey could be allowed to get into. But more than this, it is clearly contributing to the amount of stress among family members. More room might reduce family conflicts and thus give both parents more time and better time for Mikey.

   Christine's mother seems likely to be a valuable resource. She is nearby and can help out from time to time. Without her, Christine would not have been able to earn extra money by going on the buying trip to Boston. In the worst of all cases, this could have hurt Christine's relationship with the store that buys the clothes she makes. The Gordons need the money. They don't need a tighter financial situation. It also seems likely that Christine enjoys her work and takes some pride in it. Anything that reduces the stresses on Christine or makes them more manageable is good news for Mikey's interactions with his mother and thus for his cognitive development. So Mikey's grandmother is a help.

Chapter 7
Infant Social Development

LEARNING OBJECTIVES

When you have studied the material in this chapter, you will be able to:

1. Explain the sense in which newborns are <u>pre-adapted</u> to becoming social.
2. Understand what constitutes <u>sensitive</u> parental care, and the contextual factors that influence the quality of child care.
3. Outline the development of complex emotions that begin to emerge in the second half year of life.
4. Describe the formation of the attachment relationship between infant and caregiver.
5. Describe several different patterns of attachment and discuss how the characteristics of caregivers and the temperament of infants contribute to the quality of attachment.
6. Summarize the possible consequences of poor infant care and be able to suggest types of intervention that can be effective.

CHAPTER SUMMARY

I. Development in the First Half-Year

A. The Newborn as Preadapted **(pp. 212-213)**

Infants are born with a number of characteristics and abilities that help them live and develop in a social world. They have a built-in ability to signal psychological and physiological needs. Their visual system is especially sensitive to the kind of stimulation that human faces provide. They have a tendency turn their head toward sounds, especially voices.

B. The Origins of Reciprocity **(pp. 213-216)**

Soon after birth, babies appear to be socially oriented. But at this stage caregivers have to play an active part for social interaction to work well. Pacing the stimulation according to signs from the baby is an important contribution to good interaction. Being aware of a baby's feelings and needs and responding to them promptly and effectively is called sensitive care or attunement. Over time, the experience of sensitive care enables the infant to shoulder more of the responsibility for starting and maintaining social interactions.

C. Becoming an Active Participant: Social Smiling **(pp. 216-219)**

Young children are not attracted to human faces per se, they are interested in the lines and contrasts in facelike patterns. The first infant smiles occur during sleep. Waking smiles occur several weeks after birth. Adults find infant smiles powerfully rewarding and attracting. Adults tend to interpret infant smiles in terms of the baby being happy or liking them. This helps build a tie between the adult and the infant. Infants smile when they recognize familiar people or objects. Piaget described this as recognitory assimilation. At first they recognize only caregivers. By 4-5 months, they can distinguish between noncaregivers.

II. Development in the Second Half-Year

In the second half-year, the development of object permanence and a rudimentary sense of self change the infant's social world fundamentally.

A. Emotional Development **(pp. 219-225)**

Beginning at the age of 6 months, infants' emotions are associated with specific meanings. They express anger, pleasure, and surprise in relation to their own behavior and to events that they anticipate. These changes begin during Piaget's fourth stage of sensorimotor development.

Stranger Distress **(pp. 221-222).** At around 5 months of age, babies begin to smile preferentially at caregivers and react negatively to strangers. The degree of stranger distress depends on context. Distress is typically least when: 1) the stranger is at a distance, 2) the stranger is approaching the baby slowly and not intrusively, 3) the baby is in familiar surroundings, 4) the stranger's behavior is familiar to the baby, 5) the baby's mother is nearby, 6) the baby has the option to turn away from the stranger, and 7) the baby has had pleasurable experience with strangers before.

Emotions Relating to Caregivers **(pp. 222-223).** At about 9 months of age many infants begin to react negatively when their primary caregiver leaves them alone or with someone else. The onset of this separation anxiety varies across cultures.

The Beginning of Coping **(pp. 223-225).** Infants tend to cry or fall asleep in loud overstimulating circumstances. This is a coping mechanism that allows them to escape from high levels of stimulation that they cannot change any other way. After 10 months of age, infants can employ more flexible coping techniques.

B. The Development of Attachment **(pp. 225-232)**

Attachment is an enduring emotional bond resulting from countless hours of interaction between the caregiver and the infant. It is evident in the child's separation distress, joyous greeting upon reunion, and use of the caregiver as a secure base from which to explore. Infants can be attached to more than one person at a time, but not to an unlimited number. Children in orphanages may show mutual attachment to peers.

Explaining Attachment **(pp. 226-227).** John Bowlby proposed that infants are inclined to form attachments. The behaviors associated with attachment include the desire to be near the caregiver, to seek comforting upon mild stress, and to use the caregiver as a secure base from which to explore. Bowlby suggests that these once had important survival value. Evidence from research on nonhuman primates supports Bowlby's notion that attachment behavior has an evolutionary foundation.

The Quality of Attachment **(Pp. 227-230).** In the United States, about 70 percent of infants are securely attached. These babies effectively use their mother as a secure base from which to explore. They separate readily from the mother to discover a novel playroom, seek the mother out and remain with her when a threatening event is introduced, and are easily soothed by the mother's reassurance. Anxiously attached infants are less able to use the caregiver as a secure base. Bowlby proposed that different patterns of attachment reflect the differences in the infants' expectations or inner working models concerning the social world. "Working" means that the models are subject to change.

Early Day Care and Attachment **(pp. 230-232).** Research suggests that day care per se does not make a child anxiously attached. The amount, quality and timing of the child's entry into day care are each important. Low-quality out-of-home care combined with high levels of stress at home seems to be a particularly risky combination. One of the most important factors in high-quality care is the ratio of adults to children, and arrangements that allow the child to build relationships with particular day-care workers.

III. The Importance of Quality Care

A. Problems of Inadequate Care **(pp. 232-237)**

Extreme Deprivation **(pp. 232-234).** Rearing infant monkeys in isolation has severe effects on their social development. Infant monkeys raised only with peers show excessive clinging behavior and fearfulness and have trouble exploring the environment, but they are not as disturbed as isolation reared infants. Similar effects have been seen in studies of human infants raised in institutions. It is the quality of social stimulation, not just the quantity, that is important to a child's social development.

Nonorganic Failure to Thrive Syndrome **(p. 234).** The term failure to thrive is applied to infants whose growth rate is in the lowest 3 percent for their age, and to those who actually begin to lose weight. Failure to thrive is called nonorganic when no physical cause can be identified. Infants with this syndrome often have feeding difficulties. The syndrome is also associated with patterns of broadly inadequate care. The mothers of these children have been described as neglecting and even hostile. Stress, lack of social support, and the mother's childhood history may contribute to inadequate care.

Insensitive Care **(pp. 234-237).** Sensitive maternal care involves reading the infant's behavior, interpreting it correctly, and responding in a timely and appropriate manner. Insensitive care can be overcontrolling or undercontrolling. Different patterns of insensitive care are associated with different patterns of anxious attachment.

B. The Context of Care **(pp. 237-240)**

Life Stress and Social Support **(p. 237).** Social support can help people deal with stressful problems. Even inexperienced teenage mothers can raise a child relatively free of developmental problems if they have adequate support from their families.

Infant Characteristics **(pp. 237-239).** Temperament is an individual's style of responding to the world. Even very young infants have different styles of responding. Temperament characteristics are not very stable in early infancy. Belsky has suggested that measures of sensitive care predict whether infants are securely or anxiously attached, whereas measures of temperament predict behavioral differences among infants within a given attachment pattern.

The Interaction of Factors **(pp. 239-240).** Newborns' characteristics can contribute to early difficulties in parent-child relationship. This may be especially true in families under stress and without social support. Positive factors in the family environment can keep early risks from becoming stable problems.

C. Intervention and Resiliency **(pp. 240-242)**

Psychologists are quite interested in the possibility of reversing the effects of early deprivation and insensitive care. Intervention on children's social and emotional development often encounters two problems. First, even if the child is offered useful therapy, the poor quality of child care may persist and continue to exert negative influences. In addition, children with problems tend to have a negative influence on their own environments. They may isolate themselves from family and peer influences that could help sustain the benefits achieved from treatment of early problems. The most effective intervention programs are those that begin early and focus on improving both the child's behavior and its environment.

SELF-TEST

Matching: Key Terms and Concepts

1.____recognitory assimilation (p. 218)
2.____emotions (p. 219)
3.____stranger distress (p. 221)
4.____separation anxiety (p. 222)
5.____attachment (p. 225)
6.____securely attached (p. 228)
7.____anxious-resistant (p. 229)
8.____anxious-avoidant (p. 229)
9.____inner working model (p. 230)
10.____nonorganic (failure to thrive) (p. 234)
11.____insensitive care (p. 234)
12.____overcontrolling (p. 235)
13.____undercontrolling (p. 236)
14.____temperament (p. 237)

a. a product of repeated interaction

b. good balance between play and exploration

c. occurs with separation from the caregiver

d. caregiver cannot fulfill infant's need

e. caregiver's action reflects his or her own needs

f. play and exploration remain superficial

g. no physical cause

h. smile at familiar objects

i. fail to elicit social responsiveness from the infant

j. negative reactions to strangers

k. ambivalent

l. general style of responding

m. representations are subject to change

n. state of feelings

Multiple Choice Questions

1. What does it mean to say that humans are pre-adapted to become social?

   a. Infants are born with personalities.
   b. Infants have behavioral dispositions that help them participate in a social world very early.
   c. Infants are born with an urge to seek out parents.
   d. Infants can see and hear at birth.

   (Objective 1, Conceptual)

2. Which of the following tendencies is <u>not</u> characteristic of human newborns?

   a. responding to the pitch range of human speech
   b. turning their heads to a sound source
   c. attending to human eyes
   d. detecting rudimentary forms of contingency

   (Objective 1, Factual)

3. Which of the following does the term <u>attunement</u> refer to?

   a. mother coordinating her behavior with infant's
   b. mother keeping interaction slow, so infant will sleep
   c. mother distinguishing her baby's cry from the cry of other babies
   d. harmonious relationship between mother and father

   (Objective 2, Conceptual)

4. How is it that older infants are able to engage in back and forth (reciprocal) interactions with a caregiver?

   a. The caregiver creates the back and forth and the infant follows.
   b. The infant instinctively takes turns when interacting with anyone.
   c. Infants learn this skill by experiencing sensitive care and attunement.
   d. There is no real reciprocal interaction until after infancy.

   (Objective 2, Factual)

5. Why do very young babies react to a smiling and nodding human face?

   a. Babies are naturally attentive to movement.
   b. Faces have light/dark contrasts that babies are attentive to.
   c. Caregivers tend to bring their faces close to the infant to play.
   d. All of the above.

   (Objective 3, Factual)

6. Smiling in newborns is an indication of:

   a. response to line and contrast stimuli
   b. spontaneous activity in lower brain regions
   c. transition to deep sleep
   d. affection

   (Objective 3, Factual)

7. When a 2-month-old smiles more readily at mother than strangers, it is engaging in:

   a. recognitory assimilation
   b. secure attachment
   c. stranger distress
   d. separation anxiety

   (Objective 3, Conceptual)

8. Which of the following emerges along with the fourth stage of sensorimotor development?

   a. smiling when awake
   b. smiling at parents more than at strangers
   c. smiling in anticipation of coming events
   d. distinguishing smiles from frowns

   (Objective 3, Factual)

9. How do we know that 10-month-old infants evaluate strangers?

   a. They react to strangers with more complex emotions.
   b. They begin to react negatively to strangers.
   c. They are easily surprised by strangers.
   d. They are affected by context and strangers' behavior.

   (Objective 3, Factual)

10. What is activated when an infant turns its face away from an approaching stranger?

    a. a coping mechanism
    b. anxious attachment
    c. recognitory assimilation
    d. equilibration

    (Objective 3, Factual)

11. Which of the following is associated with early onset of stranger anxiety?

    a. biological differences between cultures
    b. cultural differences in parental behavior
    c. cultural differences in infant IQ
    d. biological differences in infant IQ

    (Objective 3, Factual)

12. Which of the following is a more mature pattern of coping behavior?
   a. signal the caregiver when threatened
   b. cry
   c. fall asleep
   d. turn away from the stimulation
   (Objective 3, Conceptual)

13. A good coping technique:

   a. reacts to the stimulation involuntarily
   b. can remove infant entirely from interaction with the environment
   c. helps the infant maintain contact with the environment
   d. facilitates the acceleration of heart beat
   (Objective 3, Conceptual)

14. Which of the following is <u>not</u> related to the onset of attachment?

   a. separation distress
   b. greeting upon reunion
   c. frequency of crying
   d. using the caregiver as a secure base
   (Objective 4, Factual)

15. Which of the following is necessary before true attachments can form?
   a. object permanence
   b. conservation
   c. secondary reaction
   d. cause and effect
   (Objective 4, Conceptual)

16. The formation of attachment in infancy depends upon:

   a. social interaction
   b. primate evolutionary heritage
   c. infant pre-adaptations
   d. all of the above
   (Objective 4, Conceptual)

17. The idea that attachment is biologically guaranteed implies that:

   a. even abused children are attached to their parents
   b. temperament is the prime influence on quality of attachment
   c. anxious infants lack the disposition to form attachments
   d. learning plays no role in human infant attachment
   (Objective 4, Conceptual)

18. What did Harlow's study of surrogate mother monkeys demonstrate?

    a. Attachment is biased toward figures that provide food.
    b. Attachment formation begins with a sense of security.
    c. Temperature is critical in attachment formation.
    d. Secondary reinforcement is important for attachment.

    (Objective 4, Factual)

19. What percentage of normal 18-month-old infants in the United States is attached to one or more caregivers?

    a. 100
    b. 70
    c. 30
    d. 10

    (Objective 5, Factual)

20. Which pattern of attachment is associated with reluctance to separate from the mother, even when there are interesting toys around?

    a. anxious-avoidant
    b. anxious-resistant
    c. secure
    d. both avoidant and resistant

    (Objective 5, Conceptual)

21. Which of the following statements about day care is most accurate?

    a. Early day care will make parent-child attachment anxious.
    b. Early full-time day care will not harm attachment relationships unless it is paired with family stress and poverty.
    c. Most of the day care infants who form anxious attachment display the anxious-avoidant pattern.
    d. Day care has a more detrimental effect on older children.

    (Objective 5, Factual)

22. Which of the following results from the greater complexity of human social and emotional development?

    a. more rapid development in human than monkey infants
    b. increased vulnerability to early deprivation
    c. decreased vulnerability to early deprivation
    d. closer parent-infant attachments

    (Objective 6, Conceptual)

23. Which of the following effects of early deprivation is most likely to recover if a normal environment is restored?

    a. anxious attachment relationships
    b. delayed perceptual development
    c. impaired social interaction skills
    d. delayed cognitive development

    (Objective 6, Factual)

24. What do the most effective early intervention programs involve?

    a. the earliest intervention
    b. intervention involving the environment
    c. intervention involving both the infant and its environment
    d. few early intervention programs are very effective

    (Objective 6, Conceptual)

ESSAY QUESTIONS

1. Explain what is meant by the notion that newborn s are pre-adapted to participate in a social world.

2. Explain Belsky's view of attachment and temperament as variables that influence development at different levels.

VIGNETTE HIGHLIGHT

Multiple Choice Questions

1. In the first week of Malcolm's life, he already seemed to focus his large brown eyes on everything that came into his view. What Malcolm was actually attending to was:

   a. his mother DeeDee's face
   b. anybody's face
   c. anybody's eyes
   d. light/dark contrast

2. Karen bought Meryl Oscar the Grouch from Sesame Street in his battered garbage can. When Oscar jumped up from the garbage can like a jack-in-the-box, Meryl began to cry. Karen then pushed the toy closer to Meryl. Meryl turned her head away. Karen again moved around to stay in front of Meryl's face and made the monster pop up one more time. What type of care was Karen displaying?

   a. overcontrolling
   b. anxious-resistant
   c. ambivalent
   d. undercontrolling

3. Malcolm was brought up in a large family. His grandmother, parents, aunt, and two older siblings all took part in playing with and taking care of him. To whom is Malcolm likely to become attached?

   a. his mother
   b. his grandmother
   c. his father
   d. all of the above

Essay Questions

1. Mikey was born in a family with chronic marital conflicts and financial constraints. So far, however, he doesn't seem to have been adversely affected by the conflicts in his environment. Name two positive aspects in Mikey's circumstance that may have helped him avoid some of the problems he faced.

2. Meryl was born in a single-parent family. Her mother, Karen, was too young to be responsible for a baby. In addition, Karen had a very bad relationship with her own mother. As a result, she got very little social support from her family. Name two things that could have made Karen and Meryl's circumstance a little better.

ANSWER KEYS

Matching

1. h 2. n 3. j 4. c 5. a 6. b 7. k 8. f 9. m 10. g
11. d 12. e 13. i 14. l

Multiple Choice

1.	b (p. 212)	13.	c (p. 224)
2.	c (pp. 212-213)	14.	c (pp. 225-226)
3.	a (p. 215)	15.	a (p. 223)
4.	c (p. 215)	16.	d (pp. 212, 225-227)
5.	d (pp. 212-215)	17.	a (p. 228)
6.	b (pp. 216-217)	18.	b (p. 227)
7.	a (p. 218)	19.	b (p. 228)
8.	c (p. 219)	20.	b (p. 229)
9.	d (p. 222)	21.	c (pp. 230-232)
10.	a (p. 224)	22.	b (pp. 232-233)
11.	b (p. 222)	23.	d (p. 240)
12.	a (p. 224)	24.	c (p. 242)

Essays

1. Newborns have a built-in ability to "signal" psychological and physiological needs in ways that adults can interpret and are likely to respond to:

    Newborns clearly attract social partners. For example, a newborn's visual system is naturally attentive to light/dark contrasts and to movement. As a result a newborn tends to stare at faces. Parents often interpret newborns' long looks as signs of affection.

    Newborns are pre-adapted to perceive human speech. They also have built-in coordination and will turn automatically in the direction of a voice and look at the face of the person who is speaking to them.

    Babies also tend to adapt to the patterns of care they receive. A hurried style of child care may be reflected in disrupted sleeping. An easygoing style of child care may put the baby in a regular eating and sleeping pattern (pp. 212-213).

2. Belsky has argued that temperament and quality of care may operate at different levels. He found that measures of sensitive care predict whether infants are securely or anxiously attached to their mothers. Measures of temperament predict behavioral differences among securely attached infants or among anxiously attached ones. For example, a difficult infant may cry harder than an easy infant when the caregiver leaves and show less greeting behavior when the caregiver returns. But both difficult and easy babies can be cared for in a sensitive way. And when they are, they remain temperamentally different but securely attached. Temperament differences do not imply attachment differences **(p. 239).**

VIGNETTE ANSWER KEYS

Multiple Choice

1.d (p. 212) 2.a (pp. 235-236) 3.d (p. 226)

Essay Questions

1. Although Mikey's parents are having some conflict over the issue of his mother working, they seem to have agreed on wanting to keep the marriage together and on wanting another child. In addition, both seem devoted to their children and provide Mikey with very sensitive care. It might have been much worse for Mikey if one of the parents had not wanted another child.

   A second positive aspect is the fact that they did manage to get enough money together to move into a bigger home. The financial burdens involved in this may present problems later. But for now, it is clear that much of the stress in the family will be reduced by having enough room for a family their size.

2. First, Karen's relationship with her mother might have been better if relations between her parents had been better, and if her father had been available to help with problems between her and her mother. If Karen's mother had not been under financial stress related to being a single mother, she might also have had more of a chance to teach Karen basic parenting skills that she could use with her own children.

   Second, Karen would have had an easier transition into motherhood if Meryl had not been so colicky as a newborn. Unfortunately, the stresses on Karen and her tendency toward an overcontrolling style of infant care are likely to interact with Meryl's difficult temperament in an unhappy way.

Chapter 8
Toddler Language and Thinking

LEARNING OBJECTIVES

When you have studied the material in this chapter, you will be able to:

1. Describe the characteristics of a child's first words and sentences.

2. Define the terms phoneme, morpheme, syntax, and semantics.

3. Summarize the basic rules of conversation (pragmatics).

4. Summarize the major tasks in early language learning.

5. Describe the developmental changes involved in learning the sound patterns of a language.

6. Summarize theories of how children learn the meaning of words.

7. Describe the types of syntactic rules children learn during the preschool period and suggest how they are learned.

8. Describe important characteristics of the language environment in which children learn their first language.

9. Summarize behaviorist, nativist, and cognitive perspectives on language development.

10. Summarize four perspectives on the relationship between language and thought.

11. Summarize the key limitations on a child's cognitive abilities at the end of the toddler period.

CHAPTER SUMMARY

(Pp. 257-259) The toddler period extends from ages 12 to 30 months. Toddlerhood is marked by the child's first steps and first words. The emergence and rapid development of language demonstrates three important themes in development: 1) the child's intrinsic motivation to learn and grow, 2) the biological basis for learning, and 3) qualitative changes in behaviors.

I. The Nature of Early Language

A. First Words (pp. 259-260)

When toddlers begin to speak they use single words. When these refer to an idea that adults would use several words to express, they are called holophrases. To understand holophrastic speech, it is necessary to take both context and gestures into account.

Expressive toddlers have many words for social routines. Their speech includes the use of pronouns and brief statements, such as "stop it." Referential toddlers tends to acquire words more rapidly than expressive toddlers and tend to have many words for objects and events. Their speech includes many nouns, verbs, and adjectives.

B. First Sentences (p. 261)

At approximately 18-24 months toddlers begin to put two word phrases together. The words typically refer to ideas, for example, "Daddy, car." This is known as telegraphic speech. The shortness of the sentence reflects the limited cognitive capacity the toddler has at this point in language development. Toddlers can express a wide range of ideas with these simple constructions (See Table 8.1 on page 162). Rudimentary grammatical rules are evident in toddler speech.

II. The Components of Language

(Pp. 261-262) In addition to learning specific words, toddlers must also learn conventions for combining words and rules for everyday conversation.

A. Sounds, Structures, and Meaning (pp. 262-263)

A phoneme is the smallest unit in language that can change the meaning of a word, for example, (d)og (l)og. Cross-cultural studies and studies of deaf infants show that all infants initially babble the same sounds.

Morphemes are the smallest units of meaning in language. Some words consist of a single morpheme. "Child" is one morpheme. "Unspeakable" is composed of three morphemes: un (meaning "not"), speak (meaning to say), and able (meaning possible to do).

The rules of syntax are used to combine words into sentences with the desired meaning. Knowledge of syntax is also used to understand the meaning of another person's sentences.

The term semantics refers to the meaning of language. A sentence may follow the rules of syntax and yet be semantically incorrect or meaningless (for example, "My Daddy is having a baby").

B. Conversational Rules (p. 264)

Pragmatics is the study of rules for using language properly in different social contexts. Socio-linguistics is the study of differences in language use in different social groups, classes, and ages.

C. Productive and Receptive Skills (pp. 264-265)

Productive skills are used to put ideas into words. Receptive skills enable a listener to understand what is being said. Receptive skills are acquired earlier than productive skills. Thus toddlers can understand many sentences that they could not have produced on their own.

III. Major Tasks in Early Language Learning

A. Learning the Sound Patterns of Language (pp. 265-267)

The first vocalizations are cries. Early in the first year infants begin to coo. Cooing is simply repeating vowels sounds. Babbling is the vocalization of consonant and vowel sounds together. In the babbling stage, sounds begin to resemble speech. Patterned speech consists of sounds and words based on the set of phonemes, or sounds, of the baby's language. In order to progress from cries to patterned speech, the toddler must learn to use mouth, lips, tongue, and vocal cords properly, and also learn the phonemes of its native language.

B. Learning Words and Their Meanings (pp. 267-268)

By age five, the average child may have a vocabulary of up to 14,000 words. Imitation, the use of gestures and sounds in combination, and feedback from adults when toddlers use speechlike sounds all play roles in early language learning.

The Challenge of Mastering Words **(pp. 268-269).** Toddlers make many of errors when they are learning language. Underextension errors involve applying a word (such as "truck") to a narrower range of things (only toy trucks) than it really refers to. Errors of overextension involve applying a word beyond the range of things it properly applies to. Toddlers often refer to any four-legged animal as "dog."

Theories of Word Learning **(pp. 269-272).** Toddlers' errors are important clues in language research. The semantic feature hypothesis states that the meaning of a word is acquired gradually as the semantic features or defining features of the word are acquired. This may account for underextension errors. Lexical contrast theory suggests that a toddler's current knowledge and communication needs promote attention to particular features and encourage the acquisition of new words. This may account for the decline of overextensions.

C. Learning Morphological Rules **(pp. 272-274)**

Prefixes, suffixes, and auxiliary verbs used to change the meaning of words are called grammatical morphemes. They are learned in a specific order. Both grammatical simplicity and semantic simplicity probably play a part in determining this order. The order of acquisition probably also reflects something about the general strategies used to acquire language.

That children learn rules for language rather than simply memorizing everything is clearly seen in errors they make with grammatical morphemes. Rule learning is particularly clear when toddlers apply normal rules to irregular words (for example, "mouses" instead of "mice"). This type of overregularization proves that words are not just learned by imitation.

D. Developments in Syntax **(pp. 274-275)**

Syntactic rules place limits on the way nouns and other parts of speech are used. This makes the toddler's speech more regular and predictable for listeners. Syntactic rules also give the child the productive capacity to turn even a limited vocabulary into an almost limitless number of meaningful sentences. Two areas of research demonstrate how the rules of syntax are acquired: the understanding of the passive voice and the understanding of how to construct questions.

Understanding the Passive Voice **(pp. 275-276).** Three-year-olds approach passive sentences with a semantic strategy. Four-year-olds use syntactic strategies to decode passive sentences. The use of more sophisticated strategies sometimes leads older children to make errors that younger ones do not make. These are called growth errors. By age 5 all errors of detecting the passive voice have disappeared.

Constructing Questions **(pp. 276-278).** All languages contain Yes/No questions and Wh questions (Who, What, Where, When, Why, and How). By the age of 3 children can use auxiliary verbs to construct Yes/No questions. Finally, by age 4 children are able to use tag endings to construct Yes/No questions. Wh questions are more difficult to construct than Yes/No questions. The earliest Wh questions appear at about 3 1/2 years. Even after toddlers can construct Wh questions, they often have trouble forming the negative versions of them (for example, "Why aren't you thirsty?").

E. A Closer Look at the Language Environment **(pp. 278-280)**

Adults tend to speak to children in simple sentences. They use a higher pitched voice, focus on objects and events in the present tense, and also tend to be very redundant. Fathers and mothers tend to differ in the type of child directed (motherese) language they use. After the very earliest phases of toddlerhood, this type of speech does not seem to be an important factor in the child's ability to learn a first language.

IV. General Perspectives on the Beginnings of Language

A. The Behaviorist Perspective **(pp. 280-282)**

In 1957 Harvard psychologist B. F. Skinner proposed that both vocabulary and syntax are learned by instrumental conditioning from parents and adults. Research has not supported this view. Parents do not typically reinforce sentences on the basis of grammatical correctness. Language is learned quite similarly in cultures that clearly reinforce language differently. And language acquisition proceeds much more rapidly than can be accounted for by reinforcement alone. words can be combined in ways never heard before.

B. The Nativist Perspective **(pp. 282-283)**

The linguist Noam Chomsky proposed that humans inherit a set of special language learning abilities called the language acquisition device (LAD). In support of this, he noted that language is acquired at a very rapid pace. It seems to be acquired in relatively similar fashion across different languages. And essentially every human manages to learn language regardless of IQ. Further evidence comes from the fact that there are clearly areas of the brain that are specialized for language processing. There also appears to be a critical period for language learning.

C. The Cognitive Perspective **(pp. 283-284)**

Cognitive theorists propose that language is learned through use of the same general cognitive and problem-solving abilities that children use to achieve nonlinguistic goals. That is, language is learned, but not by reinforcement or by specifically language-related learning abilities.

Cognitive theorists hold three assumptions about language acquisition. The child is an active agent in its language learning. What children understand about concepts and categories of meaning helps them to analyze the grammar of the language they hear. Language learning should be linked to the development of other cognitive skills, such as symbolic play, memory development, and block building.

V. The Relationship Between Language and Thought

A. Piaget's View (pp. 285-287)

According to Piaget, language development is just another manifestation of the general cognitive abilities acquired in toddlerhood. Most specifically, it reflects the development of representational thought.

Principal development of toddlerhood } symbolic capability = ability to let one thing stand for another that is not physically present.

B. Bruner's View (p. 287)

Harvard psychologist Jerome Bruner believes that language is more than a mere reflection of cognitive development. In his view, it plays a critical role in cognitive development.

C. Vygotsky's View (pp. 287-288)

Soviet psychologist Lev Vygotsky believed that language and thought first develop separately. Then, when children are about 2 years old, they begin to interact and influence each other. Thought processes start to affect what is said and language facilitates the integration of ideas. At that point language evolves into two components, inner speech and social speech.

communicating with others.

internalized not vocalized facilitate thinking

D. The Learning/Mediational View (pp. 288-289)

This perspective sees the first words as merely stimulus-response relationships. However, as language develops it provides verbal mediators between stimuli and responses. Verbal mediators serve to connect a stimulus to an ultimate overt response by setting up a chain of internal covert responses. Thus, the child's ability to abbreviate and internalize language helps develop thought.

E. Evaluating Different Approaches (p. 289)

It is still unclear exactly what the relationship between language and thought is. All of the above views are plausible. To adequately explain the relationship between language and cognitive development (thought), a combination of these viewpoints is most likely to provide the best explanation.

VI. The Toddler Period: An Overview

By the end of the toddler period, the child can understand the world through mental actions and manipulations. The emergence of symbolic thinking supports more elaborate social interaction, pretend play, dreams, and new approaches to problem solving. Toddlers remain limited, however, by their inability to use logic and deduction to solve problems. Symbolic thought is necessary for this, but it is not enough.

SELF-TEST

Matching: Key Terms and Concepts

1. ____motherese (p. 278)
2. ____pragmatics and socio-linguistics (p. 264)
3. ____productive and receptive skills (pp. 264-265)
4. ____holophrase (p. 260)
5. ____syntax (p. 263)
6. ____over- and underextension (p. 269)
7. ____over-regularization (p. 274)
8. ____phoneme (p. 262)
9. ____babbling (p. 266)
10. ____cooing (p. 266)
11. ____telegraphic speech (p. 261)
12. ____morpheme (p. 263)
13. ____semantics (p. 263)
14. ____grammatical morphemes (p. 272)
15. ____protolanguage (p. 267)

a. a single word used to convey broader meaning

b. speech with nonessential words eliminated

c. a single sound

d. gestures and sounds accompanied with speechlike intonations

e. smallest unit of meaning

f. prefixes, suffixes, and auxiliary verbs

g. rules of conversation

h. mouses and foots

i. the study of the meaning that language conveys

j. child-directed speech

k. two common errors in vocabulary use

l. repeating of vowel sounds

m. vocalization of vowel and consonant sounds

n. the study of rules that organize language

o. enable a child to use language

Multiple Choice Questions

1. What is the term that refers to a toddler's use of a single word to represent more than just a single object, event, or quality?

   a. holophrase
   b. morpheme
   c. phoneme
   d. babbling
   (Objective 1, Conceptual)

2. "Daddy car" is an example of:

   a. a phoneme
   b. telegraphic speech
   c. a morpheme
   d. a holophrase
   (Objective 1, Factual)

3. Which of the following refers to the smallest unit in language that can change the meaning of a word?

   a. morpheme
   b. holophrase
   c. phoneme
   d. coo
   (Objective 2, Conceptual)

4. Which of the following is the smallest unit of sound in language?

   a. morpheme
   b. phoneme
   c. holophrase
   d. coo
   (Objective 2, Conceptual)

5. What is Mother giving a lesson in when she says "Don't say 'gimme'" say 'May I please have one?'"

   a. morphology
   b. pragmatics
   c. syntax
   d. semantics
   (Objective 3, Factual)

6. The study of rules for using language in different social contexts is called:

a. pragmatics
b. socio-linguistics
c. syntax
d. semantics
(Objective 3, Conceptual)

7. Which of the following are major tasks in toddler language learning and use?

a. phonology, morphology, syntax, semantics
b. pragmatics, morphemes, holophrases, telegraphic speech
c. discourse analysis, sociolinguistics, morphology
d. location, recurrence, negation, possession
(Objective 4, Conceptual)

8. When are the sound patterns of a child's native language learned?

a. as soon as the child hears its parents speak
b. during the period of cooing
c. during the period of babbling
d. during the period of patterned speech
(Objective 5, Factual)

9. Crying, cooing, babbling, and patterned speech are all:

a. stages in acquiring the sound patterns of language
b. semantic features
c. lexical contrasts
d. sets of mental skills needed in order to master language
(Objective 5, Conceptual)

10. The idea that a toddler's current knowledge and communication needs promote attention to particular features, encourage the acquisition of new words, and cause further restrictions of overextended meanings is referred to as:

a. phonology
b. the semantic features hypothesis
c. the lexical contrast theory
d. morphology
(Objective 6, Conceptual)

11. The idea that toddlers generally learn part of a word's definition and then later the whole definition is referred to as:

    a. phonology
    b. the semantic feature hypothesis
    c. the lexical contrast theory
    d. morphology

    (Objective 6, Conceptual)

12. The use of a word in ways that do not cover all of the word's meanings is called:

    a. an error of overextension
    b. lexical contrast
    c. patterned speech
    d. an error of underextension

    (Objective 6, Factual)

13. An error that is due to the emergence of a more advanced way of thinking is called:

    a. an error of overextension
    b. an error of underextension
    c. over-regularization
    d. a growth error

    (Objective 7, Factual)

14. What type of developmental changes are involved in learning how to understand passive sentences?

    a. change from one comprehension strategy to another
    b. changes in semantic ability
    c. changes in representational thought
    d. avoiding growth errors

    (Objective 7, Conceptual)

15. Which of the following is the best predictor of the size of a child's vocabulary at age 17 months?

    a. mother's IQ
    b. baby's IQ
    c. what language the family speaks
    d. how much mother talks to baby

    (Objective 8, Factual)

16. What role does motherese play in language acquisition?

a. simplifies the comprehension task for the child
b. reinforces proper grammatical forms
c. makes the child want to be like the mother
d. teaches proper syntax
(Objective 8, Conceptual)

17. How does Chomsky think a child's language acquisition device is acquired?

a. exposure to adult speech
b. reinforcement
c. biological inheritance
d. cognitive strategies
(Objective 9, Factual)

18. Which of the following perspectives on the beginnings of language is most clearly contradicted by research data?

a. behaviorist
b. nativist
c. cognitive
d. data support all equally
(Objective 9, Conceptual)

19. The cognitive view of language acquisition differs from the behaviorist view in:

a. eliminating the role of reinforcement
b. minimizing the role of language specific learning
c. emphasizing complex rather than simple learning mechanisms
d. very little, the two models are very similar
(Objective 9, Conceptual)

20. Which of the following is Piaget's view of the relationship between language and thought?

a. Language development simply reflects conceptual development.
b. Language development causes conceptual development.
c. Language and thought are unrelated.
d. Piaget did not emphasize this in his work.
(Objective 10, Conceptual)

c 21. Which of the following theorists proposed that language and thought initially operate independently and then become coordinated?

a. Piaget
b. Bruner
c. Vygotsky
d. learning/mediation theorists
(Objective 10, Factual)

a 22. According to learning/mediational theory, language is initially:

first words = verbal responses to stimulus

a. stimulus-response ties between words and objects
b. a reflection of sophisticated language learning skills
c. a set of cognitive strategies
d. a highly specialized representational system
(Objective 10, Conceptual)

lang ↔ between stim & response

b 23. Which of the following is still not available by the end of the toddler period?

a. verbal mediators
b. logical thought
c. make-believe play
d. symbolic thinking skills
(Objective 11, Factual)

a ~~b~~ 24. Does a child leave the toddler period with a firm grasp of the difference between real and unreal or imagined things and events?

a. no
b. yes
c. only very intelligent toddlers have this
d. it depends on whether parents have taught this or not
(Objective 11, Factual)

ESSAY QUESTIONS

1. **Summarize the cognitive view of language learning.**

This view is based on the premise that cognition comes first and then the child is able to learn language to the extent that his cognitive abilities allow. This is like solving a complex puzzel. With hints etc he will figure it out. He doesn't need a special inate language ability such as an LAD (language aquisition device

2. **Compare Piaget's and Bruner's views on the relationship between language and thought.**

Piaget thought that language was a manifestation of cognitive development. And so as cognitive development took place thoughts then became expressed in words.

Bruner thought that words came first and then the thoughts are fashioned from the words the toddler knows. Language is the source of all symbolic thought.

VIGNETTE HIGHLIGHT

Multiple Choice Questions

b 1. Malcolm is heard saying "Malcky two." Mikey is heard saying "Daddy home." These are examples of:

   a. holophrastic speech
   b. telegraphic speech
   c. phonemes
   d. morphemes

a 2. Malcolm's use of "do'gin" for "do it again" is an example of:

   a. a holophrase
   b. telegraphic speech
   c. a phoneme
   d. a morpheme

d 3. Meryl's constant use of "Eh" for many objects in many situations with inflections imitating the English language is an example of:

   a. cooing
   b. babbling
   c. syntax
   d. patterned speech

Vignette Essay Questions

1. In the vignette discussions, neither Malcolm's grandmother, Mikey's father, nor Meryl's mother seem to favor motherese when talking to their children. Will this have a negative effect on the children's understanding or language development?

2. Suggest some reasons why Mikey's father, particularly, doesn't use much motherese.

ANSWER KEYS

Matching

1. j 2. g 3. o 4. a 5. n 6. k 7. h 8. c 9. m 10. l

11. b 12. e 13. i 14. f 15. d

Multiple Choice

1.	a (p. 260)	13.	d (p. 276)
2.	b (p. 261)	14.	a (p. 276)
3.	a (p. 263)	15.	d (pp. 278-279)
4.	b (p. 262)	16.	a (pp. 278-279)
5.	b (p. 264)	17.	c (pp. 282-283)
6.	a (p. 264)	18.	a (p. 281)
7.	a (p. 262)	19.	c (pp. 280, 283)
8.	d (p. 266)	20.	a (pp. 285-286)
9.	a (p. 266)	21.	c (pp. 287-288)
10.	c (p. 270)	22.	a (p. 288)
11.	b (p. 270)	23.	b (p. 289)
12.	d (p. 269)	24.	a (p. 290)

Essays

1. There are three general perspectives on language acquisition. Behaviorists believe that language is acquired in the same way as any other ability, nativists believe that the ability to acquire language is due to a unique human ability, and cognitive theorists believe that language is acquired by the use of general purpose cognitive processes.

   Cognitive theorists believe that language learning is much like solving a very complex code or puzzle. With enough hints, corrections, and repetitions, a child should be able to figure out what the code is without using anything more than everyday cognitive abilities. Cognitive theorists do not see any need for a language acquisition device or any other skills that are specifically tailored for language learning **(pp. 280-284).**

2. That representational thought and language emerge in the toddler period suggests that there is a relationship between the two. According to Piaget, cognitive development is the acquisition of general cognitive capacities and abilities. Language is just one manifestation of these cognitive changes. The ability to manipulate symbols intentionally leads to new ideas and thought. Language is just verbal manipulation of symbols. It is not an independent accomplishment or an important force in cognitive development.

   In contrast, Bruner believes that language is a crucial part of the symbolic representational system of the child. Language is the source of all symbolic thought. Language is a crucial force driving cognitive development forward. It is not merely a reflection of cognitive development.

   Developmental theorists feel that both Piaget and Bruner were emphasizing important points about language development. Language does reflect and build upon general cognitive development. But it also contributes to cognitive development, as Bruner emphasized **(pp. 285-289).**

VIGNETTE ANSWER KEYS

Multiple Choice

1. b (p. 261) 2. a (p. 260) 3. d (p. 266)

Essay Questions

1. That their parents don't use much motherese is not likely to have a lasting effect on any of the children's language development. Motherese is primarily a way of making language simpler for children when they are first starting to learn it. Much of what parents say to children can be inferred from the context in which it is said, so motherese is probably a redundant aid rather than a necessary one. Language may be learned a bit more slowly if parents do not adjust their speech to the child's level of understanding and ability to follow what is said. But eventually every healthy child learns to speak his or her native language almost flawlessly.

2. There are probably several reasons that Mikey's father doesn't use motherese very much. First of all, he is clearly interested in Mikey's developing a very masculine personality. He may think that talking to Mikey in motherese will make him act like a baby longer. That is, he may be pushing him to grow up. Mikey's father may also be uncomfortable talking this way when other adults are around, and yet may use motherese expressions with Mikey when they play by themselves. It is also possible that his background hasn't afforded him many opportunities to observe how parents adjust their speech to young children's level of understanding. Finally, it is also possible there is an element of insensitivity in his not adjusting his speech to Mikey's level of understanding.

Chapter 9
Toddler Social Development

LEARNING OBJECTIVES

When you have studied the material in this chapter, you will be able to:

1. Compare the social and emotional capacity of infants and toddlers, focusing especially on affective sharing and sense of self.
2. Recognize toddlers' need for autonomy and their sociability toward same-age children.
3. Explain the role of caregivers in facilitating toddlers' psychological growth.
4. Describe how toddlers adopt parental rules and values through the process of socialization.
5. Explain how toddlers reconcile closeness of symbiotic relationship and striving for autonomy, and how the quality of attachment and parental behaviors play a role in this process.
6. Describe the contextual factors that may influence toddlers' social development and reverse the developmental outcome from infancy.
7. Discuss the issues involved in child abuse.

CHAPTER SUMMARY

During toddlerhood children become more self-reliant and they acquire acquire rules and values from their society, through a process called socialization.

I. Two Views of Socialization

A. Socialization from the Outside **(pp. 295-297)**

Both psychoanalytic theory and early social learning theory suggest that self-control and socialization in toddlerhood are motivated by the child's desire to avoid losing the parent's affection. Contemporary social learning theorists emphasize the role of imitation and vicarious rewards and punishments in socialization.

B. Socialization from the Inside **(p. 297)**

Both our evolutionary heritage and the experience of group living bias toddlers toward becoming cooperative and sociable. Negativism in toddlerhood is an expression of a bias toward achieving autonomy. Social relationships play an important role in balancing tendencies toward compliance and autonomy.

II. Major Developments in the Toddler Period

A. Moving Out **(pp. 298-299)**

Toddlers maintain psychological contact with their caregiver not by physical closeness but by exchanging looks and vocalizing across a distance. Most 18-month-olds also show decreased distress when the caregiver temporarily leaves them.

B. Sharing of Emotional Experiences **(p. 299)**

Sharing behavior illustrates toddlers' sociability and the developing ability to see things from another person's point of view. Affective sharing involves trying to communicate the positive experience of exploration and success to caregivers who are watching or nearby. This is an example of the developing ability to coordinate thoughts, feelings, and actions.

C. Social Referencing **(p. 300)**

Social referencing is the ability to use the caregiver's facial expression or tone of voice as a cue for how to deal with novel or ambiguous situations. Social referencing can be seen in the laboratory when infants are faced with a visual cliff.

D. Active Experimentation **(pp. 300-301)**

Toddlers actively experiment with cause and effect. By doing so, they gradually integrate their various capabilities, catching the sense of executive competence. The sense that "I" can do things and the attraction toward objects help toddlers move toward greater independence.

E. Growth of Sociability **(p. 301)**

Stranger anxiety declines and behavior involving peers increases during toddlerhood. Toddler peer interactions are mostly positive in tone and often seem to include "turn taking." But such interactions are largely object-centered and can not yet be called peer "relations."

F. Awareness of Self **(pp. 302-303)**

Toddlers develop a clear understanding of the distinction between self and others. By 24 months they treat the self and others as independent agents in play. They recognize themselves in a mirror. And they use "I" and other words that show an understanding of the self-other distinction.

G. Understanding of Others **(pp. 303-305)**

One-year-olds do not understand that others are agents in their own right. By age 3, children can recognize the separateness of people's roles, intentions, and aims. Understanding of the fact that different people can play different roles and have different goals within the same game or interaction is illustrated by children's behavior in games like hide and seek.

III. Parent-Toddler Relations

A. The Parents' Task **(pp. 305-306)**

The parents of toddlers typically adjust their own behavior to match the child's current capacities and limitations. Parents set limits and also allow toddlers to try things on their own. They offer help when the child's resources are exceeded. This concept is referred to as scaffolding.

B. Fathers and Toddlers **(pp. 306-307)**

Fathers typically spend more time with toddlers than they do with infants. At every age, fathers tend to be more involved in playful behavior with children than in care and nurturance. Having two caregivers with different interactive styles may help toddlers strive for independence and ease the beginnings of psychological separation from the mother.

IV. Individual Adaptations: The Roots of Personality

A. Becoming a Separate Person **(pp. 307-308)**

Margaret Mahler discussed the development of the self in terms of separation and individuation. Newborns cannot even distinguish between sensations arising inside and those arising outside the body. By 4 months of age, babies can distinguish the caregiver from other people. By 6 months they can anticipate their caregiver's reaction and intentionally signal their needs. By the end of the first year, infants understand that the caregiver is a different person from themselves. At this point the period of symbiotic relationship ends.

B. The Challenge of the Second Year **(pp. 308-309)**

In toddlerhood, the closeness of the child-mother relationship often comes into conflict with the child's striving toward independence. A secure attachment relationship with the caregiver can help the child see that bids for self-reliance are compatible with desire for emotional partnership. In infancy, the parent's task is to be responsive and available. In toddlerhood, parents have to begin setting limits and supporting autonomy.

C. Research on the Influence of Attachment History **(pp. 309-312)**

Anxiously attached infants are likely to become clingy, easily frustrated, and prone to temper tantrums in toddlerhood. Mothers of anxious-avoidant toddlers tend to provide little help to their child and remain uninvolved in their child's activities in laboratory assessments. Mothers of anxious-resistant children offer help, but it is often lacking in clarity or timing and is difficult for the toddler to use effectively.

D. Other Factors Influencing Toddler Adaptations **(pp. 312-315)**

Temperament **(p. 312-314).** Some researchers suggest that children have unique behavioral styles that become quite stable beginning in toddlerhood. We do not yet know the relative importance of heredity and the environment in development and stability of behavioral styles. It may be that temperament affects the pacing or strength of a child's reactions, while interactions with caregivers affect the overall quality of the child's adaptations. Children's behavioral patterns can affect the parents' responses and quality of caregiving.

Family Context **(pp. 314-315).** The quality of adult relationships, the amount of stress, the various forms of social support available, and the parents' own developmental history can interact with each other and influence the quality of parent-child relationships.

V. Parental Abuse and Neglect of Toddlers

Child abuse is more common in toddlerhood than at any other age. Toddlers' self-assertion and self-competence are easily misinterpreted by parents as naughty or even malicious. Depending on the type and extent of abuse, abused children may suffer from lack of competence, avoidant attachment relationships, blunted emotions, or aggressiveness with peers.

A. Searching for Causes **(pp. 316-319)**

Child Characteristics **(pp. 316-317).** Childhood illness and irritability may play a role in child abuse by increasing stress on the caregiver. Abuse increases the risk of further illness and tends to make children even more unmanageable. Thus it is difficult to say that either the child or the adult caused the abuse.

Parent Characteristics **(pp. 317-318).** Child abuse is more likely when parents have difficulty coping with pregnancy, have limited knowledge of child care, have a history of abuse by their own parents, or are from a culture or subculture in which violence is more common than in the society generally. Mental illness is not a common cause of child abuse. Child abusers are more often "normal" parents who have trouble coping with the stresses in their environment.

The Environmental Context **(pp. 318-319).** Poverty, loss of jobs, frequent moving, serious illness, and lack of education can all contribute to child abuse. Community involvement and family cohesiveness can help prevent it. Supportive marital relationships can also help reduce the risk of child abuse.

B. Prevention and Intervention **(pp. 319-320)**

Child abuse is too complicated to be totally eliminated by any intervention program. However, early identification of mothers who are at risk for child abuse can play an important role in reducing it. Mothers who are young, poorly educated, poor, single, and socially isolated are especially at risk. When abuse has occurred, providing social support and improving the family circumstances can help prevent further damage to the child.

SELF-TEST

Matching: Key Terms and Concepts

1.____socialization (p. 294)

2.____sublimation (p. 295)

3.____affective sharing (p. 299)

4.____social reference (p. 300)

5.____executive competence (p. 300)

6.____pattern of adaptation (p. 307)

7.____separation-individuation (p. 307)

8.____symbiotic period (p. 308)

a. individual style of responding

b. coordinating with caregiver

c. acquiring the standards of the society

d. blocking and redirecting biological drives

e. becoming separate from the caregiver and aware of being an individual

f. "reading" another person's expression

g. sharing of emotional experience

h. one can use things for one's own ends

Multiple Choice Questions

1. Why are toddlers more willing than infants to play without looking at or approaching their mother when she is nearby but busy doing something?

   a. Toddlers' independence drives them away from mother.
   b. Toddlers prefer to play alone.
   c. Toddlers have longer memories than infants.
   d. Toddlers understand that mother will be responsive if needed.
   (Objective 1, Conceptual)

2. Which of the following develops in toddlerhood without much relationship to cognitive development?

   a. affective sharing
   b. executive competence
   c. using social reference
   d. all depend on cognitive development
   (Objective 1, Factual)

3. In a visual cliff experiment, 12-month-old infants were more willing to cross over the glass if their mothers smiled and encouraged them. This is an example of:

   a. social referencing
   b. affective sharing
   c. attachment relationship
   d. psychological contact
   (Objective 1, Conceptual)

4. What type of behavior suggests that 2-year-olds have a sense of self?

   a. touching their own rouge-marked nose when looking in a mirror
   b. complex syntactical structures in their speech
   c. signaling the caregiver for help
   d. both a and c
   (Objective 1, Conceptual)

5. Thirteen-month-old Mikey gradually acquired the idea that he can use things for his own ends. He has just begun to have a sense of:

   a. social reference
   b. individual adaptation
   c. executive competence
   d. zone of proximal development
   (Objective 2, Conceptual)

6. Which of the following is most characteristic of 2 year-old's social play?

a. complexity
b. emphasis on "being together" rather than "doing together"
c. unwillingness to play if mother is not nearby
d. mostly positive mood or tone in their play
(Objective 2, Factual)

7. Which of the following insure that a toddler has both space to develop and support?

a. scaffolding
b. proximal development
c. parents' setting limits
d. scaffolding plus setting limits
(Objective 3, Conceptual)

8. What effect does setting limits have on toddler exploration?

a. increases confidence to explore
b. decreases confidence to explore
c. teaches obedience but no effect on exploration
d. increases creativity
(Objective 3, Conceptual)

9. Which of the following is most true of fathers' behavior with toddlers?

a. both parents spend the same amount of time with their toddler
b. both parents behave quite the same with their toddler
c. fathers are more involved in cognitive development than mothers
d. fathers are more involved in play than care
(Objective 3, Factual)

10. Which view of socialization emphasizes blocking biological drives in order to redirect a toddler's energy toward more socially desirable goals?

a. psychoanalytic theory
b. early social learning theory
c. contemporary social learning theory
d. ethology
(Objective 4, Factual)

11. Which view of socialization emphasizes fear of losing parental affection as a motive for compliance in toddlers?

a. early social learning theory
b. ecological theory
c. contemporary social learning theory
d. Piagetian theory
(Objective 4, Factual)

12. Mikey learned how to behave with kindness when he observed his mother comforting a neighbor's child who had fallen and hurt himself. This is an illustration of:

a. sublimation
b. observational learning
c. externalization
d. reinforcement

(Objective 4, Conceptual)

13. Which of the following patterns of infant behavior is related to clinginess, dependency, and low frustration tolerance in toddlerhood?

a. secure
b. anxious-resistant
c. anxious-avoidant
d. anxious-dependent

(Objective 5, Factual)

14. As a toddler, John would typically do what his mother asked, but often complied with little enthusiasm. What type of attachment history might account for this?

a. secure attachment in infancy
b. anxious-resistant attachment in infancy
c. anxious-avoidant attachment in infancy
d. anxious-dependent attachment in infancy

(Objective 5, Conceptual)

15. Which of the following patterns of attachment is associated with maternal support that is often confusing or not easy to use?

a. secure attachment
b. anxious-avoidant attachment
c. anxious-resistant attachment
d. both avoidant and resistant patterns

(Objective 5, Conceptual)

16. Patterns of response and behavioral styles first become stable in the toddler period. What does this suggest about temperament?

a. It must be based on patterns of child care.
b. It must be biologically based.
c. It must result from parent's perceptions.
d. none of the above

(Objective 6, Conceptual)

17. The overall quality of adaptation in a toddler is primarily a product of:

a. caregiving history
b. inborn temperament
c. child-caregiver relations plus some child characteristics
d. child characteristics plus attachment effects in specific areas
(Objective 6, Factual)

18. Which of the following contextual factors is particularly important to facilitate a good parent-child relationship?

a. a supportive community
b. supportive teachers
c. economic stress security
d. good quality of father-mother relationship
(Objective 6, Factual)

19. The quality of child-mother attachment:

a. is stable after infancy
b. is stable if the child has a stable temperament
c. can change if stress in or on the family changes
d. only changes if mother resolves conflicts related to her early years
(Objective 6, Factual)

20. Children are more likely to be abused during:

a. infancy
b. toddlerhood
c. early childhood
d. adolescence
(Objective 7, Factual)

21. Toddlers are particularly vulnerable to abuse because:

a. they are constantly testing the limits parents impose
b. their assertiveness can be misinterpreted as malicious or naughty
c. they have not yet learned how to avoid parental mistreatment
d. all of the above
(Objective 7, Factual)

22. The consequences of child abuse depend on the particular form of mistreatment. What type of mistreatment is often associated with lack of competence in dealing with objects?

a. emotional unavailability
b. physical abuse
c. physical neglect
d. both a and b
(Objective 7, Factual)

23. Which of the following is most likely to yield valid data on the effects of child abuse?

    a. retrospective research designs
    b. prospective research designs
    c. cross-sectional designs
    d. interview data

    (Objective 7, Factual)

24. Which of the following factors has been found to be associated with child abuse in prospective studies?

    a. infant prematurity
    b. early irritability
    c. mental disturbance of parents
    d. mother's general attitude during pregnancy

    (Objective 7, Factual)

ESSAY QUESTIONS

1. What kind of parental behavior does setting limits refer to, and why is it important in toddlerhood?

2. What is the relationship between independence and the need for closeness and security in toddlerhood?

VIGNETTE HIGHLIGHT

Multiple Choice Questions

1. On their way home, Malcolm and his grandmother were almost robbed. Malcolm looked at Momma Jo and then looked at the strangers and said "Go away." What type of behavior was he displaying when he looked at Momma Jo?

   a. affective sharing
   b. social referencing
   c. executive competence
   d. self-assertion

2. Malcolm showed everybody the police car and shouted "Look!" Which of the following skills has to develop before a toddler can engage in this type of information sharing?

   a. taking the perspective of others
   b. internalizing adults' value
   c. social referencing
   d. self-agency

3. When Mikey was 25 months old, his parents disagreed about putting him in day care so Christine could take a full-time job. Does research indicate that day care might be harmful for Mikey's social and emotional development?

   a. day care neither harms nor helps
   b. day care is more likely to be harmful than helpful
   c. the effect depends on time spent in care
   d. at Mikey's age good quality day care would not be a problem

Essay Questions

1. Malcolm was an energetic 2-year-old. His grandmother described him as "a pile of mischief." Nevertheless, Malcolm seemed not to be a really naughty boy. Name two things that might have helped Malcolm strive for autonomy and self-assertion without becoming a problem child in the process.

2. The marital relationship was getting worse in the Gordon family. Frank could not bring enough money home. Christine was getting more involved in her career. There were also some disagreements about whether to put Mikey in day care. Suggest two things that could have contributed to Mikey's development by reducing some of the stress in the family.

ANSWER KEYS

Matching

1. c 2. d 3. g 4. f 5. h 6. a 7. e 8. b

Multiple Choice

1. d (pp. 298-299)
2. d (pp. 299-300)
3. a (p. 300)
4. a (p. 302)
5. c (p. 300)
6. d (p. 301)
7. d (p. 305)
8. a (p. 306)
9. d (p. 306)
10. a (p. 295)
11. a (pp. 295-296)
12. b (p. 296)
13. b (p. 310)
14. c (p. 310)
15. c (p. 311)
16. d (pp. 312-313)
17. c (p. 313)
18. d (p. 314)
19. c (pp. 314-315)
20. b (p. 315)
21. d (pp. 315-316)
22. c (p. 316)
23. b (pp. 316-317)
24. d (pp. 316-317)

ESSAY QUESTIONS

1. If children can be confident that their parents will impose limits when they are needed, the youngsters may then explore their capacities freely, testing how far they will reach. What is important for the child is not the specific child-rearing practice but the parents' general approach toward the child. For example, there is no evidence that the specific age of weaning or toilet training a child has a major impact on the child's development. However, there is evidence that the general quality of care parents provide does make a difference in how well a child fares **(p. 306)**.

2. Toddlers do not exclusively try to achieve self-reliance. Instead, their striving toward autonomy is balanced by bids for a continuing emotional partnership with the caregiver. If toddlers know they can reclaim the former closeness with the caregiver, they will feel free to explore their capacities to the fullest. The parents' reliability during infancy breeds a basic trust, which then enables initiatives toward independence in toddlerhood, as long as the the caregiver responds to the child's bids for autonomy with acceptance and encouragement. Self-reliance can be reduced if children are anxiously attached, if autonomy is forced upon them too early, or if bids for independence are viewed with suspicion. This compromising of self-reliance can take many forms, including timidity and continued preoccupation with the caregiver, unremitting power struggles, persistent angry interactions, lack of emotional interest in mastery, and general emotional detachment **(p. 309)**.

VIGNETTE ANSWER KEYS

Multiple Choice

1. b (p. 300) 2. a (p. 299) 3. d (pp. 230-232)

Essay Questions

1. First of all, Malcolm is securely attached to his parents and grandmother. The secure relationship gives Malcolm a strong sense of self-reliance and self-control and willingness to follow adults' rules. Although Malcolm is easily tempted to explore anything new, he is also very responsive when Momma Jo tells him to get away from things like the edge of the pool. His confidence in Momma Jo as a responsive and reasonable caregiver probably helped him develop these early forms of self-control, which balance his independence-seeking.

   Second, Momma Jo loved Malcolm but did not indulge him. She set clear and consistent limits. Malcolm probably believes that the limits set on him leave open an arena within which anything he wants to try is probably pretty safe. This gives him confidence to do things that are right up to his ability. Sometimes it gets him into things that are more than he can handle. But both his parents and grandmother recognize that he is not being "bad" when these things happen.

2. The most obvious thing that would reduce stress on the family would be a better financial situation. This might have made the disagreements about Christine's job more manageable. If the money were not so tight, Christine might have argued that her work was fulfilling and made her feel that she could do a better job as a mother. But under the circumstances, it began to sound as if the main justification for Frank letting her work was that he couldn't bring home the bacon by himself. That made it harder rather than easier for him to accept her working. Both the money from her work and her pride in succeeding might have had positive effects on Christine's behavior with Mikey.

   It might have been helpful if Christine had had good relationships with her mother and sister and could have asked them to help care for Mikey a bit. If Mikey had had more experience of separation from his mother in familiar and friendly environments, he might have had less trouble separating from his doll. Frank and Christine would have had one less thing to set off their arguments. Fewer arguments could easily have improved both parents' attitudes and moods and helped facilitate better individual and cooperative interaction with Mikey.

Chapter 10
Cognitive Development in Early Childhood

LEARNING OBJECTIVES

When you have studied the material in this chapter, you will be able to:

1. Describe how preschoolers are active participants in their cognitive development.

2. Discuss three limitations preschoolers have in cognitive thinking: the appearance-reality problem, centration, and poor skills for managing attention and memory activities.

3. Define the following conceptual tools: rules of conservation, classification, seriation, and transitive inference.

4. Describe how preschoolers selectively attend to stimuli in their environment.

5. Describe the characteristics of the sensory register, short-term memory, and long-term memory.

6. Describe the preschooler's memory abilities and limitations and define zone of proximal development.

7. Define egocentrism.

8. Identify the three cognitive factors Flavell suggests are necessary for children to overcome egocentrism.

9. Define collective monologue and summarize the preschooler's social communication abilities and limitations.

10. Define the term script.

CHAPTER SUMMARY

(Pp. 333-336) Early childhood spans the period from 2 1/2 to 5 years of age. At this age, children begin to show signs of adult cognitive sophistication. At the same time, they retain distinctive limitations. Preschoolers have difficulty taking more than one type of information or one aspect of a problem into account at once. They are also limited by their lack of knowledge about important memory strategies and how to use them.

I. General Characteristics of Preschoolers' Thought

A. Causal Reasoning (pp. 336-338)

Piaget identified four different levels of causal reasoning in the preschool period. In level four the child is beginning to interpret objects and events in terms of the same types of reasoning that adults use, with only minor limitations. Recent research has demonstrated that children's reasoning at this age may be more advanced than Piaget concluded, especially when the tasks, problems, or questions they face are simple or familiar.

B. Conceptual Tools (pp. 338-347)

Children begin to acquire four important conceptual tools in this period. Piaget referred to them as conservation, classification, seriation, and transitive inference.

Preschoolers' Understanding of Quantity **(pp. 339-343)**. A child's first knowledge of the concept of measurement and questions of "how much" is acquired in early childhood. Rules of conservation are central to this understanding. That liquid volume, number, mass, and length are unchanged by a wide range of procedures is learned slowly. Rochelle Gelman has demonstrated that children acquire number concepts and conservation in relation to small numbers before they learn to apply the same concepts to larger numbers.

Understanding Classes and Collections **(pp. 343-345)**. Grouping items on the basis of shared characteristics is called classification. Simple understanding of classes is seen in infancy. By age 2, toddlers sort objects on the basis of a shared property such as color. In Piaget's research, children could not sort items on the basis of more than one feature at a time until they were over 5 years old. Recent research indicates that even 4-year-olds can sort on two features at once, if they are given training and practice. But even then they will sort on one feature alone unless asked to do it the way they were trained to.

Understanding Ordering (pp. 345-346). Piaget believed that concepts of number and measurement depended upon the concept of seriation. Seriation involves putting objects in a logical order. Children can place small numbers of objects in order by size before they can do the same with a larger number of objects. Solutions to tasks with small numbers of objects often reflect trial and error rather than a well-learned method for ordering the objects. But even recognizing when trial and error has given the right answer indicates a beginning understanding of seriation.

Transitive Inference (pp. 346-347). Transitivity is the concept that if A is greater than B, and B is greater than C, then A must be greater than C. Piaget felt that transitive inference was not acquired until middle childhood. Recent work by Trabasso has shown that even 4-year-olds can be trained to solve simple transitive inference problems.

Summing Up (p. 347). Piaget's research concluded that preschool children were unable to solve conservation, classification, seriation, or transitive inference problems. More recent research shows that with adequate training children will show at least some ability to use these conceptual tools. But throughout early childhood, use of these concepts is limited by centration and the appearance-reality problem.

II. Preschoolers' Attention and Memory Abilities

A. Deploying Attention (pp. 348-349)

Preschoolers have difficulty selecting information, maintaining focused attention, and ignoring irrelevant stimuli. Young children lack systematic strategies for visually scanning stimuli. The first scanning strategies involve scanning from the focal point of a picture downward. Older children generally scan a picture completely, from top to bottom. The development of effective scanning strategies is an important part of learning to deploy attention efficiently.

B. Preschoolers' Memory (pp. 349-353)

Both recognition memory and recall abilities are present before the preschool period. But preschoolers often fail to recognize how memory has to be used in a given task. By the end of the preschool period, children recognize the need to remember but they may not know what to do to insure good recall. Waters and Andreassen suggest that children's initial use of memory strategies is limited, context specific, and inconsistent. As the child becomes older, strategies are used in more contexts and are used more consistently.

Vygotsky noted that at any point in cognitive development there are things the child has not learned but could if given proper training and support. Such things are within the child's zone of proximal development. Things that would be beyond the child's ability to learn at a given moment are said to be beyond the zone of proximal development.

III. Social Cognition

A. Egocentrism in Preschoolers **(pp. 353-355)**

One of the most striking limitations on children's thinking is their tendency to be egocentric. Egocentrism is the tendency to assume that everyone else sees a task or problem the same way you do. Elements of this can be seen in many different tasks and at all stages of development.

B. Communication and the Decline of Egocentrism **(pp. 355-359)**

The ability to adjust speech appropriately when playing with a child who is older or younger is an important communication skill. A child who is egocentric is less likely to make such adjustments. Egocentrism also gets in the way of children holding true conversations. At the height of egocentrism in preschoolers, they often carry on collective monologues. Another result of preschool egocentrism is that children this age are largely unable to explain stories they hear to someone else. They do not recognize that information they leave out makes the story impossible to follow. Memory limitations may be a factor in early egocentrism. Tasks that are simple or familiar make fewer demands on working memory. Children are less egocentric in such tasks.

C. Limited Cognitive Resources and Communication **(pp. 359-360)**

The ability to handle environmental complexity and engage in effective communication increases with age. As children get older things in the environment become more familiar. Children also develop clearer expectations about what is likely to happen next in a given situation. Scripts are abstract representations of a sequence of actions needed to accomplish some goal. The emergence of scripts reflects the child's increasing familiarity with how things work. When situations are familiar and predictable, less working memory is needed to monitor the environment and more is available for considering what play partners already know and what they need to know. This leads to improved communication and less egocentrism.

IV. An Overview of Preschool Cognitive Development

Preschoolers are very active in trying to understand the world around them. They seek explanations for what they see. They learn that they can use their memory strategically and they acquire powerful cognitive strategies. But significant limitations remain. Preschoolers still have a limited number of cognitive skills. They do not always understand when to use strategies or what strategies to use for a particular task. They are not very good at evaluating how efficient a problem-solving strategy is. And they continue to have trouble with the reality-appearance problem.

SELF-TEST

Matching: Key Terms and Concepts

1._____ centration (p. 335)

2._____ appearance-reality problem (p. 335)

3._____ egocentrism (p. 335)

4._____ conservation (p. 339)

5._____ seriation (p. 339)

6._____ classification (p. 338)

7._____ transitive inference (p. 339)

8._____ class (p. 343)

9._____ collection (p. 344)

10._____ zone of proximal development (p. 352)

11._____ collective monologue (p. 356)

12._____ scripts (p. 359)

a. a>b, b>c, a>c

b. a natural grouping

c. abstract representation of a sequence of actions

d. being fooled by surface appearance

e. items with shared characteristics

f. gap between actual and potential performance

g. sorting items by size and shape

h. attention to only one aspect of a problem at a time

i. inability to take another person's perspective

j. one type of egocentric speech

k. a logical progressive arrangement of items

l. understanding and knowledge about quantity

Multiple Choice Questions

d 1. In which of the following areas is the preschooler most limited?

a. exploration of the world
b. interest in explaining events
c. interest in finding general patterns and rules
d. integration of multiple pieces of information
(Objective 1, Factual)

a 2. Which of the following refers to the preschooler's inability to focus on more than one aspect of a situation at one time?

a. centration
b. classification
c. seriation
d. conservation
(Objective 2, Conceptual)

c 3. The preschool period is characterized by three main limitations on cognitive abilities. Which of the following is <u>not</u> among the limitations on preschool age thought?

a. appearance-reality problem
b. centration
c. object permanence
d. skills for managing attention and memory activities
(Objective 2, Factual)

b 4. Which of the following refers to the fact that preschoolers are easily fooled by the visual characteristics of a display?

a. centration
b. the appearance-reality problem
c. egocentrism
d. transitive inference
(Objective 2, Conceptual)

d 5. Transitive inference, seriation, classification, and conservation are all:

a. characteristics of preschool thought
b. attentional abilities
c. memory abilities
d. conceptual tools
(Objective 3, Conceptual)

6. Sorting items by size, shape, make, and color is known as:

a. transitive inference
b. seriation
c. conservation
d. classification
(Objective 3, Conceptual)

7. The ability to deduce the relationship between two objects by knowing their respective relationships to a third object is known as:

a. transitive inference
b. seriation
c. conservation
d. classification
(Objective 3, Conceptual)

8. Arranging sticks from the largest to the smallest is an example of:

a. transitive inference
b. seriation
c. classification
d. conservation
(Objective 3, Conceptual)

9. Buttons, zippers, and snaps are examples of:

a. centration
b. collections
c. classes
d. transitive inference
(Objective 3, Conceptual)

10. Which of the following developments in the preschool period provides mechanisms for controlling the transfer of information from the sensory register to short-term memory?

a. attentional skills
b. centration
c. memory skills
d. collective monologue
(Objective 4, Factual)

11. Studies of preschoolers' deployment of attention indicate that they:

a. are systematic when scanning stimuli
b. tend to scan from the focal point of the stimuli downward
c. begin scanning at the top of the stimuli and continue downward
d. both a and c
(Objective 4, Factual)

12. Information that is consciously attended to in the sensory register is moved to:

a. an awareness of need
b. the zone of proximal development
c. long-term memory
d. short-term memory
(Objective 5, Factual)

13. According to information processing theory, all immediate experience is held in:

a. the sensory register
b. the zone of proximal development
c. short-term memory
d. long-term memory
(Objective 5, Factual)

14. Which of the following is characterized by limited capacity for information and a limit on how long information can be held?
a. the zone of proximal development
b. the sensory register
c. long-term memory
d. short-term memory
(Objective 5, Factual)

15. Which of the following is characterized by an unlimited capacity for information and no limit on how long it can be held?

a. the zone of proximal development
b. the sensory register
c. long-term memory
d. short-term memory
(Objective 5, Factual)

16. Processes that control the transition from short-term memory to long-term memory are known as:

a. attentional skills
b. centration
c. memory skills
d. collective monologue

(Objective 6, Factual)

17. The gap between a child's actual performance and the child's potential performance is known as:

a. centration
b. the zone of proximal development
c. egocentrism
d. transitive inference

(Objective 6, Factual)

18. A father is speaking to his preschool daughter on the telephone and asks if she has had dinner. What is she demonstrating if she answers with a nod instead of saying "Yes" or "No"?

a. social cognition
b. knowledge of existence
c. egocentrism
d. social inference

(Objective 7, Conceptual)

19. The inability to take another person's perspective is known as:

a. centration
b. egocentrism
c. transitive inference
d. the existence of knowledge

(Objective 7, Factual)

20. Which of the following is involved in a preschool child's understanding that a parent's interests and ideas may be different than his or her own?

a. social inference
b. knowledge of existence
c. awareness of need
d. all of the above

(Objective 8, Conceptual)

a 21. Which one of the following does <u>not</u> have to be acquired for a preschooler to overcome egocentrism?

a. collective monologue
b. knowledge of existence
c. awareness of need
d. social inference
(Objective 8, Factual)

d 22. A collective monologue is one type of:

a. social inference
b. transitive inference
c. script
d. egocentric speech
(Objective 9, Factual)

d 23. Mary says, "This building is going to be very high up to the sky." Paul says, "Yeah, the cookie monster wants to take a nap." What are Mary and Paul displaying in their play?

a. appearance-reality problem
b. communication decline
c. scripts
d. collective monologue
(Objective 9, Conceptual)

b 24. Which of the following is an abstract representation of a sequence of activities and becomes available in the preschool period?

a. social inference
b. script
c. collective monologue
d. transitive inference
(Objective 10, Factual)

ESSAY QUESTIONS

1. Although preschoolers have acquired the ability to use a variety of memory strategies, they still don't have the memory ability seen in adults. What are some of the reasons for this?

They still have limited cognitive abilities. They are frequently less familiar with the information. Also, they do not have strategies to help them remember

2. How might experience with agemates help the preschool child begin to overcome egocentrism?

He/she will become able to start to

knowlege of existence { see that other people have different perspective on things. Then he will

awareness of need { learn that to get along its helpful to consider the others point of view.

Then he/she must gradually gain skill

social inference { at social inference, the ability to interprete others peoples thoughts and feelings

VIGNETTE HIGHLIGHT

Multiple Choice

A 1. Malcolm's inability to use reasoning and compromise lead him to hit April. This is an example of the poor communication skills children have, and also demonstrates the presence of:

a. egocentrism
b. collective monologue
c. conservation
d. transitive inference

B 2. Meryl's ability to assume the role of a cashier at a supermarket shows the use of:

a. collective monologue
b. scripts
c. knowledge of existence
d. awareness of need

C 3. Mikey is 3 years old. His teachers are impressed with his ability to solve problems that even 5-year-olds have trouble with. In addition, Mikey is described as being the peacemaker in his class. He always seems to be able to prevent fights between his friends. This description of Mikey points to:

a. egocentrism
b. a solution to the appearance-reality problem
c. interdependence of social cognition and cognitive abilities
d. the zone of proximal development

Essay Questions

1. Malcolm is extremely active at home and at school. Discuss the advantages and disadvantages of this in terms of his cognitive development.

advantages: He uses his time energetically learning about the world.

Disadvantage: He can get in trouble with teachers and classmates because he may not allow time to work things out.

2. Joe Turner seems to be a very calm and patient man with good sense about how to behave with a preschooler and what to expect from a child Meryl's age. He also seems to offer good advice and good examples for Meryl's mother. How might this influence Meryl's cognitive development?

This will allow Meryl to overcome her emotional problems which she had with her mother and concentrate on the cognitive part of her development.

ANSWER KEYS

Matching

1. h 2. d 3. i 4. l 5. k 6. g 7. a 8. e 9. b
10. f 11. j 12. c.

Multiple Choice

1. d (p. 334)	13. a (p. 348)
2. a (p. 335)	14. d (p. 348)
3. c (p. 335)	15. c (p. 348)
4. b (p. 335)	16. c (p. 348)
5. d (pp. 338-339)	17. b (p. 352)
6. d (p. 338)	18. c (p. 353)
7. a (p. 339)	19. b (p. 353)
8. b (p. 339)	20. b (p. 354)
9. c (p. 343)	21. a (pp. 354-355)
10. a (p. 348)	22. d (p. 356)
11. b (p. 349)	23. d (p. 356)
12. d (p. 348)	24. b (p. 359)

Essay Questions

1. A variety of things contribute to the persisting limitations on preschoolers' memory. First, although preschoolers can use a number of memory strategies fairly well, preschoolers often fail to recognize when a situation involves things that will have to be remembered. Even if they know that they need to remember, they often fail to use strategies that they know and could very well use. They are more likely to use strategies if the situation suggests strategy use and if it is like situations in which the strategy was first learned. With age memory strategies are used in a wider range of situations and with a wider range of materials than in the early years. Preschoolers' memory is also limited by their rather unsophisticated attention and search strategies. That is, even the intention to recall and the very best strategies will not give good recall if you do not attend to the material and examine it appropriately. This may account in part for the fact that preschoolers often get less benefit from using a particular strategy than an adult does. Finally, preschoolers are less likely than adults to have had extensive experience with the things and events they have to remember. They have a smaller repertoire of schemes and scripts. As this repertoire increases, the child is increasingly able to use working memory efficiently **(pp. 349-353).**

2. One of the most interesting limitations on social cognition in preschoolers is egocentrism. It is evident in preschoolers' collective monologues, in their limited ability to retell stories or events without leaving out lots of critical information, and it seems to be at the root of many of their social conflicts and problems in sharing. Social experience can help the preschoolers overcome egocentrism. First, playing with other children lets preschoolers experience egocentric behavior from peers. This can help them learn that some types of messages or replies are inadequate. If a child played only with adults, no one would ever treat him or her egocentrically and he or she might be slower in figuring out that it is necessary to give clear messages. Playing with peers also leads to some punishment of egocentric responses. At least some of the time, preschool playmates must fail to understand, ignore, or react with frustration to egocentric behavior. Adults can more easily understand what a child knows or means, and thus they may often understand and even respond appropriately to egocentric responses or requests from a preschooler. Thus, peer experience might add something beneficial to the child's progress toward becoming less egocentric. Of course, elements of egocentrism remain even in adults. But the beginning of peer relations and major declines in egocentrism do occur in the preschool period **(pp. 353-359).**

VIGNETTE ANSWER KEYS

Multiple Choice

1. a (p. 335)   2. b (p. 359)   3. c (p. 353)

Essay Questions

1. Being very active can be both an advantage and a disadvantage in Malcolm's cognitive development. On the positive side, by being active he tends to become involved in things around him and to move to new things readily. So he probably gets more exposure to new and interesting things than a child who is content to sit around or stay with the same thing all the time. Also, since he is so active, parents and teachers are pushed to give him things to keep him busy. A quieter, less active child might elicit less attention from adults and be left to sit doing nothing much more of the time. Malcolm also seems quite smart. So he doesn't seem to miss much as he flies around all day. If he were a slower learner, his fast pace might be a disadvantage since he might not put enough time into things to learn from them. On the negative side, Malcolm's pace might put some adults off. Quiet children do not make such demands on adults' energy. His high activity level may make some playmates avoid him too. It certainly gets him involved in some conflicts that might not happen if he would slow down. If teachers decide he is "hyperactive" they may begin to expect trouble from him and treat him as a problem. If this happens, teachers might focus more on controlling him than on keeping him interested in things. This could make school a less enriching and less interesting experience for him.

2. Joe Turner's way of helping Karen with Meryl and his own manner with Meryl is likely to have a positive effect on her cognitive development in several ways. First of all, he is helping Karen get better control over Meryl's behavior. The more manageable Meryl is, the more likely it is that her time with her mother will be spent in stimulating, interesting, and mutually enjoyable activities. Joe also seems to encourage Karen to have more confidence in herself and in Meryl. Both of these can have positive effects on how Karen and Meryl interact and thus on Meryl's cognitive development. Joe himself seems to be patient and interested when he plays with Meryl. Since children this age need to be given room to try things for themselves and also room to make mistakes, Joe's style is probably a good one for a child this age. He is probably a good model for Karen in this respect. Her worries about Meryl may lead her to correct her too quickly or to place unreasonable demands on her. Both of these could limit exploration, problem solving, and self confidence in ways that negatively affect Meryl's cognitive development. With Joe around, Meryl may be more likely to get the best from both Joe and her mother.

Chapter 11
Social Development in Early Childhood

LEARNING OBJECTIVES

When you have studied the material in this chapter, you will be able to:

1. Describe developmental changes in exploration and self-reliance during early childhood.
2. Describe peer relationships in early childhood and explain how to measure social competence in early childhood.
3. Define and describe ego-resiliency and the behaviors associated with it in early childhood.
4. Summarize key steps in the development of aggression, empathy, and altruism.
5. Explain the process by which children come to adopt their parents' rules and values as their own.
6. Describe the development of gender roles and sex-typed behaviors.
7. Describe preschoolers' play and discuss the role it plays in relation to later social development.
8. Describe preschoolers' developing sense of self-constancy and the formation of self-esteem.
9. Summarize parenting practices that support preschoolers' social development.
10. Explain how temperament and social experience interact to influence the child's sense of self and of the world during early childhood.

CHAPTER SUMMARY

(Pp. 365-367) The major developmental issues facing 2 1/2- to 5-year-olds are: (1) expanding their world from home to day care and preschool, (2) developing true peer relationships, (3) self-control and self-management, (4) exploring adult roles through social fantasy play, and (5) adopting norms and values by which to guide social behavior.

I. Developmental Changes in Early Childhood

A. The Child's Expanding World

Exploring the Environment **(p. 367).** Level of curiosity and exploration is a good index of each child's overall adjustment. Preschoolers who are more self-reliant and more socially competent tend to obtain higher scores on measures of curiosity.

Moving Toward Greater Self-Reliance **(pp. 368-369).** A number of skills that emerge in early childhood support the preschooler's striving for autonomy and surprising sense of power. These include improved motor skills, language and problem-solving ability, tolerance of frustration, imagination, and fantasy play. Most preschoolers ask for help when they encounter difficult problems or obstacles. This is called instrumental dependency. Preschoolers who demand great amounts of attention and physical contact are said to be emotionally over-dependent. Anxious attachment in infancy is one source of emotional over-dependence in early childhood. Emotionally over-dependent children are as curious as other children, but they need a parent's constant reassurance in order to keep exploring.

Interaction with Peers **(pp. 369-372).** Two-year-olds can sometimes engage in social turn taking. But coordinated mutual exchanges, sharing fantasies, making up elaborate rules in games, and responding to each other's questions do not emerge until the preschool years.

Assessing Social Competence **(pp. 370-372).** Both the ability to sustain the give-and-take of peer interaction and being highly regarded by peers are indications of social competence. There are three ways to measure social competence: (1) teachers' judgments, (2) playmates' or classmates' judgments, and (3) direct observation of peer play.

The Importance of Relations with Peers and Siblings **(p. 372).** Play with peers is both fun and instructive. In play, children learn concepts of fairness, reciprocity, cooperation, managing interpersonal aggression, culture norms, and sex roles. Research on isolated monkeys, orphans, and socially withdrawn children all indicate that peer play (especially with younger partners) can substantially reduce early behavior and adjustment problems. Sibling relationships are especially important because they continue over time and involve frequent and wide-ranging interactions. Both younger and older siblings profit from their relationship.

B. Self-Control and Self-Management **(pp. 373-377)**

According to Eleanor Maccoby, a number of skills related to self-control and self-regulation emerge in the preschool years. These include 1) the ability to consider consequences of current behavior, 2) the ability to delay gratification in order to obtain greater benefits later, 3) the ability tofut deal with obstacles when pursuing a goal, 4) increased control over emotions and emotional expression, 5) the ability to engage in more than one activity at a time, and 6) the ability to limit irrelevant thoughts in order to concentrate on a specific task. Ideally, a child learns to exercise different levels of self-control and restraint in different circumstances. Children who can do this are described as ego-resilient. They are neither extremely rigid nor lacking in control. Instead, they are expressive and outgoing, and yet they are patient and careful when this is more appropriate.

can control behavior to be appropriate

C. Aggression and Prosocial Behavior **(pp. 377-381)**

The development of self-regulation and self-management skills has important influences on both aggression and prosocial behavior.

Developmental Changes in Aggression **(pp. 378-379).** When angry or aggressive behavior is used to get or defend something, it is called instrumental aggression. By the end of preschool period, children have learned alternative ways to deal with possession of objects and instrumental aggression drops. Behavior aimed at causing injury is called hostile aggression.

The Development of Empathy and Altruism **(pp. 379-380).** **Empathy** is the ability to vicariously experience the thoughts and emotions of another person. **Altruism** involves acting unselfishly in order to aid someone else. They are two forms of prosocial behavior. Even infants can become distressed if they see someone else frightened or crying. But true understanding of the other person's situation and the ability to determine what would be appropriate help do not develop until early childhood. Parents' child-rearing practices have an important effect on the development of many forms of prosocial behavior.

What Influence Does Television Have **(pp. 380-381)**? There is still disagreement about the effect of television viewing on children's aggressive and prosocial behaviors. Aggressive behavior seems to be increased immediately after exposure to violent TV programs, especially in youngsters who were already rated high in aggressiveness. Ethical constraints and our inability to completely control what children see on TV have made it difficult to obtain strong evidence on long-term effects.

D. From Imitation to Identification **(pp. 381-383)**

Identification is the process by which children adopt aspects of parents' behavior, feelings, and values as their own. The cognitive sophistication necessary to infer parents' feelings and values is a prerequisite for identification. Identification is a very complex process. Consequently, most research has focused on specific aspects such as imitation. A great deal is known about the features that make a child more or less likely to imitate a model. Children are particularly likely to imitate the behavior of models that they perceive as powerful or as nurturant and warm.

E. Sex-Typed Behavior and Gender Concept **(pp. 383-385)**

Gender concept involves classifying one's self as male or female. This occurs quite early in childhood and is closely tied to cognitive development. Children with absent or ambiguous genitals can develop equally well as males or as females, if they are assigned to one gender or the other before age three. But once a child has decided that it is a male or a female, it is difficult and disturbing to attempt to convince it otherwise. Gender role involves adopting a set of behaviors that society defines as appropriate for your own gender concept. Although there may be biological influences on some aspects of male-female differences in behavior, it is clear that much of gender role behavior is explicitly taught by adults and peers.

F. Changes in Children's Play **(pp. 385-387)**

Children have intrinsic motive to play. Through playing, children learn new skills and practice old ones.

Mastery of Conflict **(pp. 385-387)**. Children often incorporate issues they are concerned about into their play. It has been suggested that this helps them confront the problems and develop strategies for dealing with them. Preschoolers often play "autonomy" games, in which they get to play the parent or leader role.

Role-Playing **(p. 387)**. In play, preschoolers can practice a variety of roles they may adopt in later life. They can be parents, workers, and helpers in a variety of situations. Children who are scored high on social competence tend to engage in more social fantasy play than less competent children.

G. Further Development of the Self **(pp. 387-388)**

Children develop both a sense of self-constancy and a sense of self-esteem. Self-constancy involves a definition of the self as the same person, even across the vast changes in physical appearance and behavior that occur between toddlerhood, childhood, and adolescence. Self-esteem is the child's evaluation of him- or herself. Family experience has a major influence on self-esteem. Self-esteem can increase or decline with development and experience. It can also be very resistant to change.

II. The Parent's Role in Early Childhood Development

(Pp. 388-391) Parents can help preschoolers strive for mastery and develop a positive self-concept by avoiding ridicule, allowing room for failures, being available but not intrusive, setting firm and age-appropriate limits, and manifesting clear roles and values in their own behavior. This type of authoritative parenting, as Baumrind called it, is more related to later social competence than either permissive or authoritarian parenting.

III. Explaining Individual Differences

Interplay of Biology and Learning **(pp. 391-392).** Biology is the source of broad differences in temperament. These interact with experience to produce different developmental outcomes. Biology is also the origin of species-specific behavior (for example, aggression in human beings), which is then encouraged or dampened by day-to-day experiences.

History of Care **(pp. 393-395).** A great deal of evidence indicates that the care a child has received in the past influences current behavior in many different domains. Working models that children form on the basis of early experience can persist and influence the child's perception of events and patterns of behavior later. At the same time, much of a child's behavior is responsive to changes in care practices. It can change for the better or for the worse. So early experience does not determine all.

IV. The Coherence of Individual Behavior

(Pp. 395-397) Although children's behaviors vary across situations, they tend to reflect coherent trends and patterns. It has been suggested that an underlying definition of "self" is responsible for this coherence. Different children's "styles" of behaviors are greatly influenced by each child's developmental history.

SELF-TEST

Matching: Key Terms and Concepts

h 1._____ emotional dependency (p. 368)

f 2._____ instrumental dependency (p. 368)

e 3._____ socially competent (p. 370)

i 4._____ sociometrics (p. 370)

K 5._____ delay of gratification (p. 375)

n. 6._____ ego resiliency (p. 377)

L. 7._____ instrumental aggression (p. 378)

P. 8._____ hostile aggression (p. 378)

J. 9._____ empathy (p. 379)

B 10._____ altruism (p. 379)

C 11._____ identification (p. 382)

O 12._____ gender concept (p. 383)

D 13._____ gender constancy (p. 384)

A 14._____ self-constancy (p. 387)

G 15._____ self-esteem (p. 388)

M 16._____ authoritative (p. 390)

a. perception of a stable self

b. acting unselfishly

c. striving to be like someone else

d. gender is permanent

e. highly regarded by peers

f. only in problem-solving situations

g. thoughts and feelings about the self

h. over-dependency

i. measuring popularity

j. vicariously experiencing emotion of another person

k. waiting to receive something better

l. aimed at possessing objects

m. responsiveness plus firm limits

n. modifying self-restraint as circumstances require

o. a sense of being male or female

p. aimed at hurting someone else

Multiple Choice Questions

1. Jenny spends most of the group activities time on her preschool teacher's lap. She is showing:

   a. secure attachment
   b. an anxious attachment
   c. emotional dependency
   d. instrumental dependency
   (Objective 1, Conceptual)

2. Children judged to be low in curiosity:

   a. explore a novel toy extensively only when the mother is not nearby
   b. explore a novel toy extensively only when the mother is nearby
   c. do not explore a novel toy extensively even if mother is nearby
   d. explore a novel toy extensively no matter where the mother is.
   (Objective 1, Factual)

3. Which of the following aspects of peer play develops in the preschool period rather than in toddlerhood?

   a. turn taking
   b. object-centered interactions
   c. exchanges of conversation
   d. coordinated mutual exchanges
   (Objective 2, Conceptual)

4. Which aspect of preschool social development is measured using sociometrics?

   a. empathy
   b. popularity
   c. identification
   d. self-reliance
   (Objective 2, Factual)

5. Which of the following is a good way to measure social competence among preschoolers?

   a. finding out about the biggest and strongest child
   b. asking for parental judgments
   c. looking for absence of peer rejection
   d. counting the frequency of solitary, parallel, and cooperative play
   (Objective 2, Factual)

6. Which children adjust better to regular classrooms if they first play with younger children in a series of special one-to-one play sessions?

   a. aggressive children
   b. rejected children
   c. withdrawn children
   d. mentally retarded children

   (Objective 2, Factual)

7. According to the developmental schedule of inhibiting actions, what is the best way for an adult to disarm a 3-year-old who has found a pistol and is pointing it at someone?

   a. Explain the situation then tell the child not to shoot.
   b. Tell the child not to shoot. Explanations will be a waste of time.
   c. Tell the child not to shoot and grab the pistol.
   d. Distract the child's attention and grab the pistol.

   (Objective 3, Conceptual)

8. Which of the following is the correct statement about preschoolers' ability to delay gratification?

   a. They can delay gratification now to get a better reward later.
   b. They cannot delay immediate gratification.
   c. They can delay gratification, but only with adult prompting.
   d. They can wait if they fully understand the reward involved.

   (Objective 3, Factual)

9. Mikey suggested playing with blocks in order to resolve a fight between Justin and Bryan concerning the possession of the blocks. Mikey's behavior is an example of:

   a. empathy
   b. altruism
   c. redefining a frustrating situation
   d. authoritative ability

   (Objective 3, Conceptual)

10. John is a loud and active child, but he walks as quietly as possible when his newborn sister Mary is taking a nap. What is this an example of?

    a. empathy
    b. delay of gratification
    c. self-esteem
    d. ego-resiliency

    (Objective 3, Conceptual)

11. Ellen punched a playmate in the stomach. When the playmate complained, "That hurt!" Ellen laughed and punched her again. What type of aggression is this?

a. instrumental aggression
b. hostile aggression
c. defensive aggression
d. offensive aggression
(Objective 4, Conceptual)

12. Which of the following is demonstrated by the ability to understand or share the thoughts and emotions of another person?

a. empathy
b. altruism
c. ego-regulation
d. social competence
(Objective 4, Conceptual)

13. Which of the following is the least effective way to teach children prosocial behavior?

a. Explain the effects of negative behavior, from the victim's view.
b. Scold the child for hurting others.
c. Model nurturance and helpfulness in your behavior.
d. Speak with commitment about wanting prosocial behavior.
(Objective 4, Factual)

14. The best evidence indicates that viewing television violence increases aggressive behavior:

a. in all children
b. only in children rated high in aggression before the exposure
c. only in children rated low in aggression before the exposure
d. only in girls
(Objective 4, Factual)

15. When do preschoolers begin to identify with their parents' behavior and values?

a. as soon as parents begin pressing them to obey
b. they imitate but are still too young to begin to identify with them
c. when they sense the limitations of their own skills and independence
d. as soon as they acquire a gender concept
(Objective 5, Factual)

A 16. What type of parent is a preschooler least likely to imitate?

a. hostile but not dominant among other adult models
b. hostile and dominant among other adult models
c. warm and powerful
d. warm and firm
(Objective 5, Factual)

A 17. Which one of the following statements about gender is most correct?

a. Gender concept involves acquiring a sense of being male or female.
b. Sex differences in play behavior are biologically determined.
c. Gender concept is the cause of most sex-typed play behavior.
d. Mothers and fathers stress gender concept equally in child rearing.
(Objective 6, Factual)

C ~~A~~ 18. A baby boy with ambiguous genitals was mistakenly identified as a girl. What is most likely to happen if his parents decide to raise the child as a boy from this point on?

a. The child will accept the new sexual identity easily.
b. The child might have some problems at the beginning, but will eventually identify himself as male.
c. It is unlikely that the reassignment will be accepted.
d. Outcome depends on the child's attachment to its parents.
(Objective 6, Conceptual)

C 19. During fantasy play Mikey pretends that "The boy's mommy drove the truck and ran over him." He is using play to:

a. express forbidden behavior
b. gain the power that parents have
c. master fears and conflicts
d. identify with his parents
(Objective 7, Conceptual)

C 20. Which of the following is related to high levels of social fantasy play?

a. elaborateness of play
b. flexibility of play
c. social competence
d. aggression
(Objective 7, Factual)

21. Three-year-old Janet climbs on a chair to reach the candy jar on the kitchen counter. When her mother reprimands her she steps down from the chair and apologizes in order to reinstate the positive tone of the interactions with her mother. This illustrates the emerging sense of:

a. self-constancy
b. self-esteem
c. self-reliance
d. self-control
(Objective 8, Conceptual)

22. According to Baumrind, parents who are nurturant and do not set firm limits can expect their children to become :

a. cheerful and aggressive
b. withdrawn
c. self-resilient
d. cheerful and impulsive
(Objective 9, Factual)

23. Suomi found that monkeys isolated from others during infancy show the emergence of aggression toward peers:

a. earlier than the usual time
b. at the usual time
c. later than the usual time
d. not at any time
(Objective 10, Factual)

24. When dealing with anxious-resistant children, preschool teachers tend to:

a. accept immature behavior
b. exercise little control
c. get angry easily
d. expect compliance
(Objective 10, Factual)

ESSAY QUESTIONS

1. Summarize the major developments in self-control and self-management that occur during early childhood.

The child at first needs help to control him/her self. Then as he/she gets older he/she is able to pastpone rewards and also control him/her self

2. Define the concepts of self-constancy and self-esteem and explain how they are related.

Self constancy is the knowlege that one is the same person even after going through different experiences; such as a fight with a family member. Self esteem is what thoughs you have about yourself. So if you have a sense of self-constancy you feel sure of your self and therefore you are able to have a good feeling about yourself which is self-esteem.

VIGNETTE HIGHLIGHT

Multiple Choice Questions

A 1. Malcolm had trouble waiting when his mother was trying to take his picture. What was this an illustration of?

a. inability to inhibit actions
b. inability to delay gratification
c. poor conflict resolution
d. lack of prosocial behavior

A 2. Malcolm and April got into fight for the possession of the blue tricycle. What type of behavior does this illustrate?

a. instrumental aggression
b. hostile aggression
c. negative personal intent
d. true aggression

B ~~D~~ 3. Mikey's teacher fondly called him the class peacemaker because he was always successful at defusing trouble. Which of the following skills was Mikey using most effectively?

a. fantasy play
b. redefining frustration
c. inhibiting action
d. empathy

Essay Questions

1. Although they had a very bad start, Meryl and her mother's circumstances seemed to be much better by the time Meryl was turning 4. Identify two major improvements in their circumstances.

Joe came into their lives & helped Karen deal with Meryl

The caretaker, Mrs. Jasper, helped Meryl.

2. The atmosphere of the Gordon household has often been colored by quarrels and anger. The unstable family life had already had some negative influences on 4-year-old Mikey. Christine's bad relationship with her mother and the parents' tendency to involve the children in their conflicts are two particularly unfortunate problems in their situation. Indicate why these might have a negative impact on Mikey.

To be a mediator between parents is too much for a young to child to take on.

ANSWER KEYS

Matching

1. h 2. f 3. e 4. i 5. k 6. n 7. l 8. p

9. j 10. b 11. c 12. o 13. d 14. a 15. g 16. m

Multiple Choice

1. c (p. 368)	13. b (p. 380)
2. b (p. 369)	14. b (p. 380)
3. d (p. 369)	15. c (p. 382)
4. b (p. 370)	16. a (p. 382)
5. d (pp. 370-371)	17. a (pp. 383-384)
6. c (p. 372)	18. c (p. 384)
7. d (p. 374)	19. c (p. 385)
8. c (p. 375)	20. c (p. 387)
9. c (p. 377)	21. a (pp. 387-388)
10. d (p. 377)	22. d (p. 390)
11. b (p. 378)	23. b (p. 392)
12. a (p. 379)	24. a (p. 395)

Essay Questions

1. By age 2, most children show at least preliminary efforts at self-control. Developments during the toddler and preschool years fall into four related areas. (1) Inhibiting actions: Preschoolers develop the ability to understanding adults' instruction as well as to inhibit a response. By age 2 1/2, children's capacity for inhibiting impulses tends to be fairly consistent across different situations. (2) Delaying gratification: Although preschoolers can delay gratification much more effectively than toddlers, they are still easily attracted by the availability of immediate rewards. They cannot delay as well as older children without help or prompting from an adult. (3) Tolerating frustration: By preschool age, most children have acquired the social skills and strategies to deal with minor frustrations in an adaptive way. Instead of beginning a tantrum, they may ask for adults' help, turn away, or redefine the situation so the problem no longer exists. (4) Adjusting self-control to the situation: By the end of early childhood there are clear individual differences in children's ability to adjust self-control to different circumstances. Most children can adjust levels of self-control so that they are appropriately outgoing or (for brief periods at least) quiet as a situation requires. But by this age, there are clearly some children who are proving to be deficient in this area **(pp. 373-377).**

2. Self-constancy means the perception of a stable self, a self that endures despite varied behaviors and varied responses from others. It is a natural product of long-term interaction between children and their parents. Children with the sense of self-constancy know what parents expect from them and are aware of their own thoughts and motivations. Although all children come to acquire a sense of self-constancy, not all come to think of the self in exactly the same way. The particular view of the self based on each child's unique experiences is referred to as self-esteem. Developmental psychologists suggest that favorable self-esteem stems from a history of positive exchange with others **(pp. 387-388).**

VIGNETTE ANSWER KEY

Multiple Choice

1. a (pp. 374-375) 2. a (p. 378) 3. b (p. 377)

Essay Questions

1. The most obvious improvement involves the benefits of Karen's new relationship with Joe. First, the relationship has direct benefits in terms of promising very effective new social support for Karen, both in her personal life and in her parenting. These indirectly benefit Meryl. In addition, it is a fact of life today that a couple with a child is more likely to manage financially than a single mother. If the household finances improve with Joe on the scene, this will reduce stress on both Karen and Meryl.

Second, Joe is not only a supportive marital partner but a sensitive caregiver. He plays with Meryl, reads to her, and sets clear and firm limits for her behavior. His responsive, firm, and reasonable disciplinary style has set a good model for Karen and also changed Meryl's perception of how to cope with frustration. The consistency of the disciplinary style would eventually change Meryl's inner working model of the world and help her head to a better developmental outcome.

expectations about how others are likely to respond to them.

2. Christine's bad relationship with her mother has several costs attached to it. It deprives Christine of an important source of social support. It is a source of stress on her and the family. And it puts limits on the kind of relationship Mikey can have with his grandmother. Both the stress and the lack of social support can affect Mikey by affecting Christine's parenting in negative ways. And although child-grandparent attachments are not essential to the child's development, they can be a source of important social learning. So Mikey is likely to be missing something here.

The parents' tendency to involve the children in their disagreements can have two negative effects. First, it increases the children's exposure to the conflicts and to their parents' ineffective ways of dealing with disagreements. Second, it may make the children feel that they are somehow responsible for the fights and make them feel guilty. Both of these effects can influence the working models of self and of relationships that Mikey develops. As a result, negative effects on his personality and behavior could persist even if the parents' conflicts were resolved and did not reappear.

Chapter 12
Cognitive Development in Middle Childhood

LEARNING OBJECTIVES

When you have studied the material in this chapter, you will be able to:

1. Describe cognitive advances and limitations in middle childhood.
2. Define metacognition.
3. Describe development in understanding Piagetian conservation concepts in middle childhood and define contingent and necessary truth.
4. Summarize the information-processing analysis of conservation concepts.
5. Define the terms hierarchical classification, matrix classification, and class inclusion.
6. Define constructive memory, mnemonic strategies, and metamemory and indicate how they are related to memory development in middle childhood.
7. Define scaffolding.
8. Define intelligence quotient and reaction range.

CHAPTER SUMMARY

(Pp. 411-415) Middle childhood is marked by the refinement and more widespread use of cognitive abilities that emerged in early childhood. Middle childhood is also characterized by emergence of the ability to think systematically and to use multiple pieces of information at one time. This opens the door to major improvements in the child's ability to think about thinking (metacognition) and to plan effective problem solving strategies. At the end of middle childhood, most of the remaining limitations on a child's thinking are related to 1) limited knowledge and experience, 2) the fact that sophisticated cognitive strategies are still relatively new and need practice to improve, and 3) inability to apply cognitive skills to hypothetical or abstract circumstances or data.

I. Major Cognitive Developments of Middle Childhood

A. Concepts of Conservation **(pp. 415-423)**

Most children acquire conservation of physical quantities (number, length, liquid, volume, area, mass) by the end of middle childhood. Acquisition of these concepts marks the transition from preoperational to concrete operational thought.

Mastering Conservation: An Overview **(pp. 415-418).** By about age 7 children attain a full understanding of the Piagetian conservation concepts. The child understands compensation, constant identity, and the nothing added or subtracted criterion. In addition, conservers understand the concepts of necessary truth and contingent truth.

Alternatives to Piaget's Theory **(pp. 418-421).** According to information-processing theorists, children acquire conservation skills by modifying the rules they use in conservation tasks, rather than by the kind of global cognitive reorganization Piaget emphasized. Siegler and Robinson (1982) propose five rules that that are the basis for understanding number conservation. Cooper (1984) has proposed a progression of three rules that correspond to stages in solving addition and subtraction problems. Although the information-processing approach describes the behavior of children at different ages in very clear terms, it does not explain how children construct and organize these new rules into effective problem solving systems.

Can Conservation Be Taught **(pp. 421-423)**? American psychologists believed that Piaget's theory would be contradicted if children could be taught advanced concepts in this way. Jerome Bruner demonstrated that some conservation tasks can be acquired early if the child does not actually observe the transformation of the test materials. Conservation of number has also been taught successfully to nonconservers. It is clear that younger children have more trouble acquiring conservation by direct teaching. Thus Piaget's theory has been neither decisively confirmed nor contradicted.

B. Classification Skills **(pp. 423-429)**

Hierarchical Classification **(pp.423-426).** Hierarchical classification is used to organize bodies of knowledge into classes and subclasses. It is assessed using class inclusion tasks. Children younger than 6 typically fail this task because they have difficulty thinking about a subclass and its superordinate class at the same time, unless the objects and relationships involved are ones they are familiar with from daily experience. The abstract concepts that underlie classes and hierarchies are not mastered until about age 11. Only then can a child confidently handle classification problems regardless of the objects involved.

Matrix Classification **(pp. 426-429).** Matrix classification involves classifying objects on more than one dimension (for example, color and shape) at once. Young children focus on one dimension and ignore any others. Preschoolers often start the first items in a set on one dimension and then sort the rest on second dimension. Most children master matrix classification by age 9. The game of twenty questions also involves matrix classification skills. An early strategy used in this game is called hypothesis scanning. It is eventually replaced by a more sophisticated constraint-seeking strategy.

C. Memory Abilities **(pp. 429-434)**

Basic Processes **(pp. 429-430).** Basic memory processes include the most fundamental aspects of remembering things, the routine acts of storing and retrieving information. These processes help the infant recognize familiar and unfamiliar stimuli and help toddlers recall their first words. Development in basic processes of memory continues in middle childhood, but not as significantly as in the infancy through preschool years.

Knowledge **(pp. 430-431).** One of the most interesting aspects of memory is that it involves constructing the recalled information from facts we know about the world, rather than from a stored memory trace. The amount of world knowledge a child has clearly influences this type of constructive memory. The key process in constructive memory is inference. Although constructive memory is present in the preschool years, it does not fully develop until middle childhood and continues to develop in later years.

Mnemonic Strategies **(pp. 431-433).** The word mnemonic comes from the Greek word meaning memory. Rehearsal (repeating material over and over so it is not forgotten) is a powerful mnemonic strategy that keeps information from leaving short-term memory. Other types of memory strategies that emerge in middle childhood are the tactics of organizing, classifying, and summarizing information. By the age of 10, children begin to utilize strategies consistently and effectively.

Metamemory **(pp. 433-434).** Metamemory is knowledge about memory and memory processes. It includes the individual's knowledge of his or her weaknesses and strengths in remembering and the ability to monitor his or her own memory performance on a task. Younger children are poor rememberers and also tend to be overly optimistic in estimating how much they can remember. Metamemory increases with age and seems to be an important factor in learning and using memory strategies successfully.

II. Social Interaction and Cognitive Development

A. What Children Can Learn from Children **(pp. 435-437)**

Peer interaction can reduce egocentrism and lead to the generalization of skills to new situations. Jerome Bruner proposed the term scaffolding to refer to the way in which social partners influence and support cognitive growth. It involves observing the learner's behaviors, providing guidance, hints, or advice, and offering feedback about the performance as well as correction when needed. Scaffolding requires metacognitions about what others think and understand.

B. Age, Interactions, and Learning **(pp. 437-438)**

Both didactic and collaborative learning emerge in middle childhood. Younger children tend to take part in symmetrical collaborations. Older children are able to plan long-term collaborative projects, engage in more elaborated and extended arguments, offer more effective teaching approaches, and adjust the guidance they provide as teachers. Child teachers tend to focus simply on getting their learners to accomplish the task they have to teach. They focus less on providing underlying information about the task, and in general are less effective than adult teachers.

III. Individual Differences in Intelligence

A. Conceptions of Intelligence (Pp. 438-441)

Informal Concepts of Intelligence **(pp. 438-439).** Six- to 9-year-olds view intelligence as the ability to perform difficult tasks. Ten- to 13-year-olds view intelligence as the ability to acquire information and make an effort to learn. Children 14 and older see intelligence as having two components: abstract skills and verbal skills. Abstract skills are skills that enable someone to solve problems, reason, and exercise common sense. Verbal skills are skills that reflect one's vocabulary level and accumulated information.

Formal Concepts of Intelligence **(pp. 439-441).** Alfred Binet viewed intelligence as a broad general capability. Spearman also viewed intelligence as a general capability which he called "g." Their contemporaries, French, Guilford, and Thurstone, and many recent theorists, argue that intelligence is composed of several different independent abilities. Thurstone believed that intelligence is composed of seven primary abilities: verbal meaning, inductive reasoning, perceptual speed, number facility, spatial relations, memory, and verbal fluency.

B. Exploring IQ Differences **(pp. 441-448)**

<u>IQ, Heredity, and Environment</u> **(pp. 441-444).** Both heredity and environment influence the IQ of a person. <u>Reaction range</u> refers to the limits within which the environment can influence the activity of a gene.

<u>Predicting a Child's IQ</u> **(p. 444).** Mental tests for use with infants and toddlers, such as the Bayley, Gesell, and Cattell scales, rarely predict later IQ very well. In contrast, IQ tests administered in middle childhood typically predict adult IQ quite well. The explanation for this difference is probably that the early tests and tests for older children and adults are not measuring the same thing.

<u>The Issue of Cultural Bias</u> **(pp. 445-447).** A person's performance on an IQ test depends in part on knowledge of the culture in which the test was developed. One assumption that underlies purportedly culture-fair tests such as the Raven Progressive Matrices is that intelligence can be measured with materials that do not refer to any cultural context at all. Developmentalists tend to view intelligence as closely tied to context. Thus IQ tests can afford a basis for comparisons within a culture, but they must be interpreted with special caution when they are used across cultures.

<u>IQ and Performance</u> **(pp. 447-448).** Performance on an IQ test is a good predictor of performance in school. Beyond this, IQ tests have not proved to be very good predictors of happiness as an adult, general achievement, or job satisfaction.

SELF-TEST

Matching: Key Terms and Concepts

1. ____reversibility (p. 413)
2. ____metacognition (p. 414)
3. ____compensation (p. 417)
4. ____necessary truth (pp. 417-418)
5. ____contingent truth (pp. 417-418)
6. ____primitive rule (p. 421)
7. ____hierarchical classification (p. 423)
8. ____matrix classification (p. 423)
9. ____class inclusion (p. 424)
10. ____hypothesis scanning (p. 428)
11. ____constraint seeking (p. 429)
12. ____constructive memory (p. 430)
13. ____mnemonic strategies (p. 431)
14. ____rehearsal (pp. 431-432)
15. ____metamemory (p. 433)
16. ____scaffolding (p. 436)
17. ____fluid intelligence (p. 439)
18. ____crystallized intelligence (p. 439)
19. ____mental age (p. 440)
20. ____intelligence quotient (p. 440)
21. ____reaction range (p. 443)
22. ____culture fair test (p. 446)

a. recall of new information
b. math problem solving rule
c. each question is a single self-contained hypothesis
d. limits on genes' expression
e. cognitive memory aids
f. knowing there is no change in quantity despite transformations
g. ability to think about thinking
h. aspect of a conserver's thinking
i. ability to add classes
j. peer support for learning
k. test of hierarchical classification
l. facts based on logical necessity
m. narrowing alternatives
n. empirically based facts
o. ability to multiply classes
p. avoids cultural biases
q. test of thinking and reasoning
r. knowledge about memory
s. measurement of what a person knows
t. MA/CA x 100
u. average of people with a given IQ test score
v. repeating in order to remember

Multiple Choice Questions

1. Understanding that no real change has occurred in quantity despite a transformation is called:

   a. compensation
   b. reversibility
   c. metacognition
   d. classification
   (Objective 1, Conceptual)

2. The ability to think about thinking is called:

   a. constant identity
   b. compensation
   c. reversibility
   d. metacognition
   (Objective 2, Factual)

3. Which of the following is <u>not</u> a justification used by conservers?

   a. compensation
   b. constant identity
   c. primitive rule
   d. nothing added or subtracted
   (Objective 3, Factual)

4. A way of understanding based on empirical information is known as:

   a. contingent truth
   b. necessary truth
   c. constant identity
   d. hypothesis scanning
   (Objective 3, Factual)

5. Information derived from or confirmed by logical necessity is known as:

   a. hypothesis scanning
   b. constant identity
   c. contingent truth
   d. necessary truth
   (Objective 3, Factual)

6. Which of the following is not a rule used by children to solve addition and subtraction problems?

a. primitive
b. hypothesis scanning
c. qualitative
d. quantitative
(Objective 4, Factual)

7. Organizing buttons by size and color is an example of:

a. matrix classification
b. hierarchical classification
c. hypothesis scanning
d. constraint seeking
(Objective 5, Conceptual)

8. Organizing domesticated cats, cougars, and lions under one grouping is an example of:

a. constraint seeking
b. matrix classification
c. hierarchical classification
d. hypothesis scanning
(Objective 5, Conceptual)

9. Which of the following is a task used to assesses hierarchical classifcation?

a. reversibility
b. compensation
c. constraint seeking
d. class inclusion
(Objective 5, Conceptual)

10. Using questions each having a single, self-contained idea to solve a problem is known as:

a. hypothesis scanning
b. constraint seeking
c. compensation
d. class inclusion
(Objective 5, Conceptual)

C 11. Using questions that systematically narrow down the range of possible solutions to a problem is known as:

a. hypothesis scanning
b. class inclusion
c. constraint seeking
d. compensation
(Objective 5, Conceptual)

C 12. Routine acts of storing and retrieving information are called:

a. metamemory
b. memory strategies
c. basic processes
d. knowledge
(Objective 6, Factual)

D 13. Which of the following refers to the information accumulated through experience?

a. memory strategies
b. basic processes
c. metamemory
d. knowledge
(Objective 6, Factual)

B 14. Which of the following involves recalling new information that is only partly the product of the actual data just processed?

a. fluid intelligence
b. constructive memory
c. rehearsal
d. scaffolding
(Objective 6, Conceptual)

A 15. Which of the following refers to cognitive devices for improving memory?

a. mnemonic strategies
b. constructive memory
c. fluid intelligence
d. compensation
(Objective 6, Factual)

C 16. Which of the following keeps information in short-term memory?

a. constructive memory
b. fluid intelligence
c. rehearsal
d. crystallized intelligence
(Objective 6, Factual)

B 17. Knowledge about memory and memory processes is called:

a. fluid intelligence
b. metamemory
c. constructive memory
d. crystallized intelligence
(Objective 6, Factual)

D 18. Observing the learner's behavior, providing guidance, hints, advice, and offering feedback about performance are all examples of:

a. metamemory
b. fluid intelligence
c. constructive memory
d. scaffolding
(Objective 7, Conceptual)

B 19. Analogy problems, series completion tasks, and problems in classification measure:

a. metamemory
b. fluid intelligence
c. crystallized intelligence
d. constructive memory
(Objective 8, Conceptual)

C 20. Tests of vocabulary size, general information, and reading comprehension measure:

a. metamemory
b. fluid intelligence
c. crystallized intelligence
d. constructive memory
(Objective 8, Conceptual)

D 21. Tommy answers 21 items correctly on an IQ test. The average age of children answering 21 items correctly on the same test is equal to Tommy's:

a. constructive memory
b. metamemory
c. chronological age
d. mental age
(Objective 8, Factual)

A 22. Which of the following is equal to MA/CA x 100 ?

a. intelligence quotient
b. reaction range
c. fluid intelligence
d. crystallized intelligence
(Objective 8, Factual)

C 23. The limits within which the environment can modify the effects of a gene is referred to as the gene's:

a. qualitative rule
b. constraint seeking
c. reaction range
d. quantitative rule
(Objective 8, Factual)

B 24. Culture free or culture fair tests were created to:

a. assess the contributions of heredity and environment to intelligence
b. avoid cultural bias
c. assess cognitive ways of facilitating memory
d. assess the ability to add classes
(Objective 8, Factual)

ESSAY QUESTIONS

1. Summarize Piaget's description of the stages in acquiring conservation (for example, conservation of liquid volume). Be sure to mention the types of justifications used by conservers, and also include definitions of necessary and contingent truth.

Stage 1 non conservers - see only one aspect - height.
4 years (centration)

Stage 2 5-6 yrs. - transistional - aware they may be wrong

Stage 3 7 yrs. - mature conservation
first use contingent truth - which is based on counting - use senses

compensation

then use necessary truth - which is base on logical necessity.

constant identity

nothing added or substracted

2. Describe the major advances and limitations of a child's cognitive abilities in middle childhood. Be sure to mention reversibility and metacognition.

Child advances very much but still

Limits → lacks amount of knowledge adult has.
cognitive strategies new to them.
cannat reason abstrctly

Advances:
think systematically
consider multiple pieces info simulaneously
no longer fooled by superficial appearance of objects
aquire reversibility & related conservation concepts.
meta cognition - think about thinking
cognitive strategies

VIGNETTE HIGHLIGHT

Multiple Choice Questions

1. Malcolm Williams is clearly quite an intelligent child at age 9. He also tends to channel his interests into many different activities, rather than into school or into a few well-developed interests. What does all this suggest about his school performance?

    a. High IQ predicts little about his grades.
    b. High IQ predicts higher than average grades.
    c. He doesn't apply himself, so his grades are probably lower than those of other children with the same IQ.
    d. Despite his IQ, he doesn't apply himself, which predicts poor grades.

2. When Meryl's mother got into the real estate business, Meryl enjoyed looking at the houses in her mom's catalogues. By now Meryl probably has basic classifications skills down fairly well. Which of the following ways of grouping houses would be an example of matrix classification of houses?

    a. organizing houses by size and location
    b. ranking houses by cost
    c. dividing houses into single family and multiple family, single-family urban and single-family rural, and urban with garage versus urban without garage
    d. rating houses in terms of attractiveness and then in terms of cost

3. If 6-year-old Mikey and his dad had gone fishing and caught three fish, which of the following would most likely have surprised Mikey when they got home?

    a. finding four fish in their bucket
    b. finding longer fish in their bucket
    c. finding heavier fish in their bucket
    d. finding the water level in the bucket was higher with the fish in the bucket than it was before they were put in

Essay Questions

1. Malcolm is quite bright. He would probably do well on standardized IQ tests, especially in comparison to other children in his immediate neighborhood. At the same time, he is still very active and doesn't seem to stay with any one thing very long. Suggest one thing in Malcolm's school environment that could make this combination of intelligence and high activity a problem for Malcolm.

a rigid teacher who doesn't value creativity

2. Even at age eight Mikey imagines that his parents' marital problems and divorce were partly his fault. Since he has a number of relatively sophisticated cognitive skills by this time, why does he make this mistake?

1. he's still egocentric

2. parents problem too abstract

ANSWER KEYS

Matching

1. f 2. g 3. h 4. l 5. n 6. b 7. i 8. o 9. k 10. c 11. m

12. a 13. e 14. v 15. r 16. j 17. q 18. s 19. u 20. t 21. d 22. p

Multiple Choice

1. b (p. 413)	13. d (p. 430)
2. d (p. 414)	14. b (p. 430)
3. c (p. 417)	15. a (p. 431)
4. a (p. 417-418)	16. c (p. 431-432)
5. d (p. 417-418)	17. b (p. 433)
6. b (p. 421)	18. d (p. 436)
7. a (p. 423)	19. b (p. 439)
8. c (p. 423)	20. c (p. 439)
9. d (p. 424)	21. d (p. 440)
10. a (p. 428)	22. a (p. 440)
11. c (p. 429)	23. c (p. 443)
12. c (p. 429)	24. b (p. 446)

Essay Questions

1. There are three stages in the acquisition of conservation. In the first stage children are limited by centration. Children use a consistent rule to judge quantity. This rule is generally incorrect, but they are content using it time and time again. Stage two is a transitional period. Children often make errors in conservation but they also seem to recognize that something is wrong and they try to understand what it is. This is a sign that they are no longer totally centering on one dimension of the problem at a time. In stage three children become conservers. They can use compensation, constant identity, and nothing added or subtracted justifications to answer quantity problems. The ability to conserve also shows the child's ability to understand necessary truth. This is truth based on logical necessity. Necessary truth is different from contingent truth. Contingent truth is factual information based on empirical proof **(pp. 416-418)**.

2. In middle childhood children begin to think systematically and consider multiple pieces of information simultaneously. This ability is acquired as a result of the decrease in centration. Resolving the appearance-reality problem, children are no longer fooled by the superficial appearance of objects. They also acquire reversibility and understand related conservation concepts. Finally, children now think much more effectively about their own knowledge and thought processes. This ability to think about thinking is called metacognition. It is an important part of developing cognitive strategies. However, there are still limitations in children's thinking. They still lack the broad base of knowledge that adults have. Second, most of their cognitive strategies are new to them. They will improve with practice. Last, children still cannot reason maturely about abstract and hypothetical problems. Their reasoning is restricted to concrete concepts **(pp. 413-414)**.

VIGNETTE ANSWER KEYS

Multiple Choice Questions

1. c (pp. 444-446) 2. a (pp. 423-429) 3. a (pp. 415-417)

Essay Questions

1. One thing that might lead an intelligent but very active child into problems would be a teacher or school curriculum that involved lots of strict control over the class, lots of sitting at a desk doing repetitive work sheets, penalties for misbehavior rather than rewards for doing all the work, and a large number of children per class. He probably would not have the level of self-control required, and the teacher would probably be too busy to keep him busy and interested. He would be punished when he finished work ahead of other children and began to jump around. Over time the boredom, inability to meet teacher demands, lack of reward for academic successes, and frequent penalties from the teacher would tend to outweigh even his parents' desire for him to like school and to do well. This would be unfortunate because the same intelligence and quickness could be turned into real advantages in a different classroom environment.

2. Although Mikey is much more cognitively sophisticated than he was in early childhood, there are still some major limitations on his ability to reason about complex matters like his parents' marital situation. First of all, even at this age, children still have a tendency to think egocentrically in the face of complex problems. So Mikey may think of himself as the cause of things that he was not responsible for. Second, Mikey can only apply his cognitive skills to relatively concrete problems. The parents' problems are too abstract for him to work with. And even if they were not, he would still be handicapped by the fact that his knowledge base regarding the types of problems they were dealing with would be very limited. When cognitive strategies and reasoning skills are first acquired, they are most easily applied to topics that the child knows a lot about.

Chapter 13
Social Development in Middle Childhood

LEARNING OBJECTIVES

When you have studied the material in this chapter, you will be able to:

1. Define self-concept, social self and social comparison.
2. Explain the relationship between self-esteem and locus of control.
3. Explain the importance of the peer group as a developmental context in middle childhood.
4. Discuss the importance of friendships and popularity in school-age children.
5. Describe the characteristics of aggressive and prosocial behaviors in middle childhood.
6. Discuss the importance of sibling relationships in the family.
7. Summarize a multidimensional model of parenting.
8. Discuss the possible consequences of marital conflict and divorce for school-age boys and girls.
9. Describe the impact of school education, including its relationship to gender role learning.

CHAPTER SUMMARY

(Pp. 451-453) Freud described the period from 6 to 12 years as the latency period. He felt that early sexual urges became quiet at this point, only to reawaken at the beginning of adolescence. Erik Erikson noticed the importance of striving for skills and accomplishment at this age and suggested that it leads to a sense of industry. Developmental problems in middle childhood would lead to a sense of incompetence and inferiority. During this period children also integrate all their roles into a coherent self-concept, develop true friendship and mutual trust with peers, and begin to understand the meaning of being a member of a group and conforming to group norms.

I. Development of the Self

A. Advances in Self-Understanding (pp. 454-457)

From the Physical to the Psychological Self **(pp.454-456).** Before middle childhood, children distinguish themselves from others in terms of physical attributes and physical activities. By the early elementary school years, they begin to distinguish themselves from others in terms of thoughts and feelings. Selman called this an inner private self.

Development of the Social Self **(pp. 456-457).** The social self defines "who I am" in the view of "many other people around me." School children begin to have the ability to define themselves in terms of how they appear or try to appear to others (for example, "I am friendly"). They also begin to include social group membership in their self-description.

The Self in Comparison with Others **(p. 457).** Although young children are sensitive about getting their fair share of rewards, they do not evaluate their successes and failures in terms of other children's achievements until they are about 7 or 8 years old. They do not use these social comparisons systematically until they are 9 or 10 years of age. Social comparison sharpens the definition of self in middle childhood.

B. Self-Esteem in School-Age Children (pp. 457-458)

Self-esteem can be measured by asking children for overall ratings of satisfaction with who they are, or by asking specific questions about self-attitudes, skills, and accomplishments. Quality of adaptation in infancy and preschool years predicts level of self-esteem in middle childhood. Self-esteem tends to be quite stable and is a good predictor of a child's confidence in approaching the world, success in school, and confidence in his or her values and ideas.

C. Locus of Control and Self-Management **(pp. 458-459)**

A person who views him- or herself as very effective and believes that success depends on resources "within" oneself would score very high on tests measuring internal locus of control. Low scorers are said to have an external locus of control. The idea that you are responsible for your own physical and cognitive successes emerges before the understanding that social successes can also depend on your own actions. Preschoolers tend to think that whether a person likes or does not like them is due to external factors, rather than to their own behavior. Children with internal locus of control exert better self-discipline and self-management, as shown in delayed gratification tasks.

II. Peer Relations

(Pp. 459-460) The word peer means "on equal standing." Control over aggression and ideas about reciprocity and equity are important developmental outcomes that are significantly influenced by experience in the peer group. Peer relations are also a context in which children learn how to communicate their ideas and feelings to others and continue to overcome egocentrism.

A. Developmental Changes in Peer Interaction **(pp. 460-465)**

Advances in Communication Skills **(Pp. 460-461).** Unlike preschoolers and early elementary age children, fifth- and sixth-graders are quite good at taking a listener's knowledge into account when they describe an object or event. They are also quite good at indicating what extra information they need when they fail to understand something someone tells or explains to them.

Changes in Prosocial and Aggressive Behavior **(pp. 461-462).** Instrumental aggression declines as communication skills and perspective taking skills increase. But some forms of hostile aggression increase in middle childhood. In particular, advanced social understanding and self-understanding enable children to invent effective forms of verbal aggression, including a wide range of insults designed to distress or offend playmates.

Changes in Peer Friendships **(pp. 463-465).** Children's concepts and expectations about friendships develop rapidly during middle childhood. The capacity for reciprocal support and loyalty emerges. When children this age are asked why they are friends with particular children, they now cite personality characteristics such as honesty, kindness, and sociability. Younger children tend to explain friendships in terms of what the peer can do or what he or she owns. Relationships between friends become quite different from any relationships between acquaintances at this age. Friendships are characterized by common interests, harmony, humor, and depth of involvement.

B. Peer Groups in Middle Childhood **(pp. 465-471)**

Elementary school children tend to play with relatively stable clusters of friends called peer groups. At this age, peer groups are strongly segregated by gender. Girls tend to have one or two best friends and stress intimacy and the sharing of confidences. Boys tend to have larger peer groups with an emphasis on loyalty and shared activities.

Developing a Sense of "Groupness" **(pp. 465-467)**. Preschoolers have only rudimentary feelings of "we" versus "they." The concept of group boundaries and membership develops in middle childhood, along with changing conceptions of the self and others. Sherif and his colleagues illustrated the sense of groupness in their famous study of elementary age children in summer camp.

Adherence to Peer Group Norms **(pp. 467-468)**. Elementary school children are very concerned about enforcing their peer group's rules of conduct (norms). They especially emphasize fairness (equity) and conformity to the rules in games. School-age children do divide things unequally at times, but they tend to justify this in terms of who is most deserving rather than in terms of selfishness. Conformity to the peer group declines toward the end of middle childhood, especially in situations in which the peer group's behavior violates personal norms.

Socialization Within the Peer Group **(pp. 468-469)**. Interaction with peers is an important context for learning cultural norms and values. This is especially true of gender-related norms. Children ridicule and tease playmates who violate gender segregation norms. This process may protect young children from premature sexual contact.

Status and Popularity in the Peer Group **(pp. 469-471)**. The quality of care received earlier in childhood influences a child's behavioral style with peers. Popularity and peer group status are good predictors of leadership and enjoyment of peer play. Popularity in third grade has even been related to mental health records examined eleven years later.

III. Family Influences on Development

A. Sibling Relationships **(pp. 471-473)**

Sibling relationships often involve age differences and male-female pairings that are not seen very often in middle childhood friendships.

Emotional Qualities of Sibling Relationships **(p. 472)**. Children typically have very positive views of their older brothers and sisters. Older siblings can be very nurturant of younger siblings, while at times resenting their demands for attention and their access to parental attention. The ability to make social comparisons, which emerges in middle childhood, is a source of many sibling conflicts. Parents can have a major influence on how well siblings get along. The quality of sibling relationships seems to be stable at least over a period of a few years.

What Siblings Learn from Each Other **(pp. 472-473).** Older children practice role taking, nurturant behavior, and teaching skills in sibling relationships. Younger children benefit by having multiple attachment figures within the family and opportunities to practice negotiation skills.

B. The Impact of Parents **(pp. 473-483)**

When children reach middle childhood, the focus of effective parenting changes from controlling and directing to monitoring and supervising. This involves giving the child more responsibility, using more reasoning, and following the rule of equity and fairness.

Parenting Styles and Their Influences **(pp. 474-478).** Parenting styles are often described in terms of two dimensions, love versus hostility and control versus autonomy. Various patterns of these dimensions are related to different patterns of child behavior. Parenting styles tend to be stable across situations and siblings. When parental behavior is changed, behavior problems can be reduced.

Gender-Role Teaching by Parents **(pp. 478-481).** Parents of school-age children tend to tolerate and encourage independence and exploration in boys. Girls are often encouraged to stay close to home and become involve in domestic activities. Boys are typically rewarded for showing ambition and assertiveness; girls are rewarded when they are nurturant and loving. In the early elementary years, children follow gender stereotypes very closely. Toward the end of elementary school, conceptions of gender role become more flexible.

Parental Conflict and Divorce **(pp. 481-483).** The effects of parental divorce are either greater or easier to detect than in boys than girls. Some children do not experience negative effects. Many negative effects attributed to divorce may actually be due to a history of family conflict, rather than to separation from the parents after the divorce. A warm and close relationship with at least one of the parents can reduce the effects of parental conflict and separation on elementary school age children.

Effects of Parent-Child Separation **(pp. 482-483).** The effects of parent-child separation depend on the child's age and sex, the behavior of the custodial parent, and the degree to which the absent parent manages to remain involved.

IV. Children in School

Children learn mainstream cultural norms and values from their classmates. Schools not only emphasize traditional gender roles, they often reward patterns of competition and achievement that boys have been oriented toward. Many American schools unintentionally and subtly discourage intellectual achievement in girls. Rutter's extensive survey found a strong relation between the quality of school education and students' scholastic achievement and social adjustment.

SELF-TEST

Matching: Key Terms and Concepts

H 1.____latency period (p. 452)

G 2.____sense of industry (p. 452)

E 3.____social self (p. 456)

J 4.____internal locus of control (p. 458)

C 5.____external locus of control (p. 459)

B 6.____peer groups (p. 465)

A 7.____(peer group) norms (p. 467)

F ~~A~~ 8.____authoritative (p. 476)

I 9.____authoritarian (p. 476)

D ~~A~~ 10.____agency (p. 476)

a. rules of conduct

b. agemates

c. success is from luck

d. tendency to take initiative

e. personal identity as affected by other people

f. setting limits but being willing to compromise

g. Erikson

h. Freudian theory

i. using punishment

j. success is from personal efforts

Multiple Choice Questions

C 1. Having a child judge his or her overall self-satisfaction and personal talents provides us with a measure of:

a. self-understanding
b. self-management
c. self-esteem
d. the social self
(Objective 1, Factual)

B 2. What kind of evidence would a 6- to 8-year-old typically give as his or her reason for saying that he or she is a person, not a dog?

a. no reason, just insist he or she is a person
b. physical features that distinguish him or her from dogs
c. personality characteristics that distinguish him or her from dogs
d. cite mother or father as having said he or she is a person
(Objective 1, Conceptual)

C 3. School age children begin to recognize that what people say and do is not necessarily what they think and feel. This involves the concept of:

a. social self
b. locus of control
c. inner, private speech
d. social comparison
(Objective 1, Conceptual)

D 4. Jamie says, "I play piano better than Lucy." What skill is Jamie using?

a. social self
b. internal locus of control
c. external locus of control
d. social comparison
(Objective 1, Conceptual)

B 5. Nine-year-old Jack thinks he received an A on his exam because of "luck." Which of the following orientations does this illustrate?

a. internal locus of control
b. external locus of control
c. internal self-esteem
d. external self-esteem
(Objective 2, Conceptual)

6. When do children begin to form true peer relationships?

a. in toddlerhood
b. during the preschool years
c. during the elementary school age years
d. in adolescence
(Objective 3, Factual)

7. Which of the following statements about Sherif and Sherif's (1953) study of boys' sense of groups is not true?

a. At first, there was anger and changing leadership inside each group.
b. The game series fostered a strong sense of group identity.
c. The game series fostered prejudices and hatred between the groups.
d. The game series facilitated cooperation between the groups.
(Objective 3, Factual)

8. How does conformity to the peer group change during the elementary school years?

a. It is stable.
b. It decreases.
c. It increases.
d. It is unstable.
(Objective 3, Factual)

9. Which type of child is most likely to be found playing alone?

a. a rejected child
b. an ignored child
c. a neglected child
d. a popular child
(Objective 3, Factual)

10. Which of the following statements is not true of ignored children?

a. They usually stand on the sidelines and do not participate.
b. They tend to engage in negative behavior such as aggression.
c. They are rejected by peers.
d. They do things that maintain their "ignored" status
(Objective 3, Factual)

11. Which of the following is true of girls' peer groups in middle childhood?

a. They tend to be larger than boys' groups.
b. They tend to involve one or two best friends.
c. They are highly competitive.
d. They are likely to include boys and girls.
(Objective 3, Conceptual)

12. When do children first begin to form friendships based on mutual trust and support?

  a. in toddlerhood
  b. during the preschool years
  c. during the school age years
  d. in adolescence

(Objective 4, Factual)

13. Which of the following statements is <u>not</u> true of school age children's frienships?

  a. Pairs of friends are almost always cooperative.
  b. Children who become friends easily find shared interests.
  c. Friends show more positive emotion.
  d. Friends are more concerned with how rewards are distributed.

(Objective 4, Factual)

14. Which of the following would an elementary school age child cite to justify splitting a reward unequally with a friend?

  a. age difference
  b. gender difference
  c. performance difference
  d. depth of friendship

(Objective 4, Conceptual)

15. Which of the following increases as schoolchildren acquire wider social understanding?

  a. instrumental aggression
  b. competition
  c. mixed-gender play groups
  d. verbal aggression involving insults

(Objective 5, Factual)

16. Aggressive children are more likely to interpret others' actions as having hostile intent. Which of the following predicts these "errors of interpretation"?

  a. secure attachment
  b. resistant attachment
  c. avoidant attachment
  d. ambivalant attachment

(Objective 5, Conceptual)

17. Which one of the following is an older brother not likely to learn in interactions with his younger brother?

    a. non-egocentric communication
    b. teaching skills
    c. nurturance
    d. role taking

    (Objective 6, Factual)

18. Which of the following is true of sibling relationships?

    a. They are basically just friendships.
    b. They differ from friendships in terms of age, gender, and duration.
    c. They are more harmonious than friendships.
    d. They negatively affect an older child's attachment to parents.

    (Objective 6, Conceptual)

19. Which of the following is most commonly used, along with restrictiveness versus permissiveness, to describe patterns of parenting?

    a. warmth versus hostility
    b. secure versus anxious
    c. anxious overinvolvement versus calm detachment
    d. cognitive versus social

    (Objective 7, Factual)

20. Preschoolers who are energetic and self-reliant tend to be raised by parents who are:

    a. authoritative
    b. authoritarian
    c. permissive
    d. democratic

    (Objective 7, Factual)

21. Changing child rearing practices of parents with problem children will likely lead to the child's adjustment being:

    a. unchanged
    b. better
    c. worse
    d. briefly improved, followed by deterioration

    (Objective 7, Factual)

22. If you wanted to predict the effects of parenting on child behavior, which of the following would be the most useful strategy?

a. Assess one parenting style in great detail.
b. Assess parenting style from the child's point of view.
c. Assess more than one dimension of parenting in the study.
d. Limit the study to families with two parents in the home.

(Objective 7, Conceptual)

23. Which of the following might explain why the relationship between behavior problems and divorce is relatively weak?

a. Behavior problems arise from family conflict, not divorce.
b. Boys are more likely to be affected by divorce than girls.
c. Girls' behavior problems are difficult to detect.
d. The relationship is not weak, it is strong and consistent.

(Objective 8, Factual)

24. Who is more likely to fit the stereotype of the "model student" in today's schools?

a. boys
b. girls
c. children with very high IQs
d. stereotypes are avoided in modern schools

(Objective 9, Factual)

ESSAY QUESTIONS

1. Explain the relationship between self-esteem and locus of control in middle childhood.

Locus of control = person feels he/she is in control and grades etc. are obtained by ones efforts

self esteem — to think well of yourself, you need to know that your efforts bring you success
take credit. (when do good.)

2. Summarize the two-dimensional model of parenting described by Baumrind (1967).

warmth vs hostility
control vs. autonomy

VIGNETTE HIGHLIGHT

Multiple Choice Questions

A 1. That Malcolm did not dare to show his fondness toward Tammy reflects a strong sense of ____________ among school-age children.

   a. peer group norms
   b. social self
   c. social comparison
   d. external locus of control

B 2. Which of the three families in the vignettes is likely to make the most persistent effort to train every detail of gender-appropriate behavior in their child?

   a. Malcolm Williams's family (DeeDee, John)
   b. Mikey Gordon's family (Christine, Frank)
   c. Meryl Polonius Turner's family (Karen, Joe)
   d. most families emphasize gender related behavior equally

C 3. When one of the boys turned Malcolm in for having a knife at school, Malcolm attributed it to bad luck and to the fact that the boy who turned him in was white. What do these feelings reflect?

   a. hostile aggression
   b. instrumental aggression
   c. external locus of control
   d. social norms

Essay Questions

1. That Malcolm was caught carrying a knife could have had serious consequences. Name two important things in Malcolm's school and family environments that prevented this from becoming a major negative experience.

family - stood behind him
school - was reasonable and gave him another chance

2. By third grade, Meryl appeared shy and withdrawn only when it came to strangers and new situations. Her family situation had improved and she had established two new and important relationships, one with her baby brother Joey and one with her best friend Amy. Explain how Joey and Amy may have led to improvements in Meryl's social behavior.

children learn from other children
Amy - friend - control agression, friendship - trust, honesty, loyalty, support
Joey - nurturance, etc

ANSWER KEYS

Matching

1. h 2. g 3. e 4. j 5. c 6. b 7. a 8. f 9. i 10. d

Multiple Choice

1. c (pp. 457-458)	13. a (p. 464)
2. b (p. 455)	14. c (p. 467)
3. c (p. 456)	15. d (p. 462)
4. d (p. 457)	16. c (p. 462)
5. b (p. 459)	17. a (p. 473)
6. b (p. 453)	18. b (p. 471)
7. d (p. 466)	19. a (p. 475)
8. b (p. 468)	20. a (p. 476)
9. a (p. 469)	21. b (p. 476)
10. b (p. 469)	22. c (p. 475)
11. c (p. 465)	23. b (p. 481)
12. c (p. 453)	24. b (p. 484)

Essay Questions

1. Locus of control and self-esteem are related in two ways. First, high self-esteem involves confidence in one's own abilities. This expectation of success supports the idea that success is due to your own efforts rather than to luck or other people's help. At the same time, internal locus of control contributes to high self-esteem by making you ready to take credit whenever you do have successes. A child with an external locus of control is likely to dismiss successes as accidental or the result of luck. Thus, the attributional style termed internal locus of control and the self-evaluation termed high self-esteem are different concepts but they act to support one another **(pp. 457-459, 485)**.

2. Degree of warmth versus hostility and degree of control versus autonomy are the key dimensions in Baumrind's model. She has defined authoritative parents as those who are warm and responsive but firm in discipline. They tend to have self-reliant and socially competent children. Authoritarian parents are harsh in their discipline and rigid in enforcing rules. They tend to have irritable, conflict-ridden, aggressive, or socially withdrawn children. Children raised by permissive parents, who are nurturant but unwilling to set firm limits, tend to become cheerful and friendly but also impulsive and undercontrolled **(pp. 476, 390)**.

VIGNETTE ANSWER KEYS

Multiple Choice

1. a (p. 467) 2. b (pp. 404-409) 3. c (p. 458-459)

Essay Questions

1. First, the schoolteacher established good contact with Malcolm's parents. Some teachers would not have felt able to go to the parents. In these cases, the issue is resolved in the principal's office rather than at home. Malcolm's parents helped by being willing to work with the teacher rather than becoming angry or automatically defending Malcolm. Without this, the teacher would not have had confidence that they would do anything about the problem. Cooperation between the school and the parents makes it possible to monitor and correct a child before he or she is labeled a problem and begins to associate with problem peers.

Second, Malcolm's parents handled their end of the problem very well. They did not scold him or use physical punishment. Instead, they explained why it was wrong to carry a knife. It was also useful to take the knife away, not to prevent Malcolm from taking it to school again, but to show that they were serious about setting limits and caring about his behavior. The goal was to remind Malcolm about the rules he had to impose on himself rather than on their power to make him obey if they wanted to. This an effective parenting style for school-age children. At this age, monitoring and correcting does more than parental control to teach responsibility.

2. First, Meryl learned a lot about child care, nurturance, and household responsibilities after the baby was born. She also learned about sharing her parents' attention. The relationship between Meryl and her parents had also changed because of the younger sibling. The new family member could have been a big problem for Meryl's development. However, her parents understood her special needs and responded appropriately. Their sensitivity minimized problems and made the baby an asset instead.

Meryl's friendship with Amy was a typical school-age girls' friendship, emphasizing mutual trust, loyalty and support. This type of relationship is likely to enhance Meryl's understanding of self and others. In addition, the experience of being liked and playing with Amy probably also enhanced her self-esteem. It probably reduced her focus on parents a bit as well.

Chapter 14
Physical and Cognitive Development in Adolescence

LEARNING OBJECTIVES

When you have studied the material in this chapter, you will be able to:

1. Describe the biological changes that children experience in adolescence.
2. Describe the cognitive advances made in adolescence.
3. Describe Piaget's theory of formal operations.
4. Discuss the various criticisms that have been leveled at Piaget's theory of formal operations.
5. Define imaginary audience and personal fable.
6. Describe Piaget's theory of moral reasoning.
7. Describe Kohlberg's theory of moral reasoning.

CHAPTER SUMMARY

(Pp. 501-503) Adolescence is the period between 13 and 18 years of age. Until the 20th century, adolescence was seen as much like adulthood. The biological changes and physical transformations of adolescence significantly influence cognitive and social development.

I. Biological Changes During Adolescence

A. Puberty: Norms and Individual Differences (p. 504)

Generally, puberty begins about two years earlier for girls than for boys. The onset of puberty is influenced by heredity, nutrition, level of stress, and amount of exercise. Menarche is the onset of menstruation for girls and the ability to ejaculate mobile sperm for boys. The statistically normal range for girls is from 9 to 16 years of age, and for boys from 10 to 19 years. Very early onset or very late onset of puberty may result in psychological stresses for the adolescent. Historically, improved health and nutrition seem to have lowered the age of onset of puberty in the United States, although this decrease appears to have stabilized.

B. Hormonal Control of Puberty (pp. 505-506)

Sexual development begins even before birth and continues through puberty. In boys, increased secretion of androgen at puberty produces live sperm and secondary male sex characteristics. In girls, increased secretion of estrogen produces menstruation and secondary female sex characteristics. Some researchers believe that increased production of sex hormones is triggered by the level of melatonin produced by the pineal gland. Others suggest a critical weight hypothesis, which states that menarche occurs at a relatively constant weight in girls. In addition, growth spurts in both sexes are weight-related. Changes in the metabolic rate in the body are thought to be the mechanism for this.

C. A Closer Look at the Physical Changes of Puberty (pp. 506-511)

Changes in Appearance **(pp. 506-509).** Secondary sex characteristics include changes in skeletal size and proportion, new distributions of muscle and fat tissue, growth of hair on certain body parts, and such specialized changes as the lowering of the male voice. Tanner (1962) has proposed five stages in the development of pubic hair and genitals (see Table 14.1, p. 507). There is a great deal of variation in the rate of development in boys and girls, but typically girls show the first signs of physical maturation (Tanner's Stage 2) between 10 1/2 and 13 years and boys reach this stage between 12 1/2 and 14 1/2. Adolescents also experience a growth spurt. This begins at about 10 1/2 for girls and 12

1/2 for boys. Males and females have different patterns of skeletal growth. Males tend to have broader shoulders, narrower hips, and longer legs relative to the torso than females. Growth stops when increased amounts of sex hormones cause calcification of the cartilage. Increases in weight, strength, and endurance also occur in adolescence.

Changes in Brain Structure and Function **(pp. 509-511).** Hormonal changes during adolescence may result in structural changes in the brain. These in turn may be related to some of the cognitive changes seen in adolescence. Supporting data include the young child's abilities to learn another language easily; young children's ability to recover relatively easily from brain injuries; and a decrease in the amount of deep sleep during adolescence. Increased brain weight around puberty could be the result of increased numbers of neurons, the brain's nerve cells, and the decrease in synapses, connections among neurons in the brain. All of these changes reflect the brain's increased efficiency in functioning but also its decreased flexibility. This may be related to the decrease in fluid intelligence in mid-adolescence, and the gradual increase in crystallized intelligence through adolescence into adulthood.

II. Changes in Thinking During Adolescence

(Pp. 511-513) Piaget viewed adolescence as qualitatively different from other periods of development, with adolescent thinking being fundamentally different from childhood thinking. Other researchers focus on the continuity with past cognitive skills. All agree that adolescence marks the beginning of mature reasoning and problem-solving capabilities. Piaget described changes in thought at this age in terms of the emergence of formal operational thought. This involves logical reasoning about abstract concepts and systematic thinking. The ability to think about relationships among concepts leads to the capacity for hypothetico-deductive reasoning, introspection, improved metacognition, and the ability to understand such abstract concepts as justice, religion, and society.

A. Exploring Piaget's View of Adolescent Thought **(pp. 513-521)**

After watching children performing a variety of scientific problem solving tasks, Piaget concluded that adolescents approach and understand such problems in different terms than elementary school children. Consult your text for descriptions of the law of floating bodies study and the balance scale study, which show the ability to reason about proportion; the bending rods study and the pendulum study, which show the ability to isolate variables that may have an effect on results; and the all-possible-combinations study, which shows the ability to combine a number of different factors in a systematic way.

Piaget makes three general conclusions about this stage of development. First, the sophistication of adolescent thought about hypothetical and abstract concepts reflects the emergence of formal operations. Second, the flexibility of adolescent thought arises from new relationships among mental operations, rather than from the addition of new operations alone. These operations can be organized in terms of two logical models: the system of 16 binary operations and the INRC group. The system of 16 binary operations involves the adolescent's ability to take two variables and consider them simultaneously, e.g., long vs. short length and heavy vs. light weight. The INRC (identity, negation, reciprocity, and correlativity) group refers to the ability to see relationships between variables. In Piaget's view, this explained the use of broader logical relationships in adolescence and the ability to manipulate conclusions and produce deeper meanings. Piaget concludes that formal operations are new and qualitatively different from previous operations. Nonetheless, the same processes of adaptation and equilibration that produce earlier cognitive structures also produce formal operations.

B. Is Piaget's View Correct? **(pp. 521-524)**

(Pp. 521-522) Researchers agree that Piaget's description of adolescent thinking is quite accurate. His tasks do a good job of sampling the range of thinking skills that emerge in adolescence. However, his theory of how these skills develop has received a great deal of criticism. His models of concrete and formal operations appear to be incomplete and unclear, and new models are required to better describe this period of development. Despite this, Piaget's model provides the basic organizational framework for contemporary research in this area.

How Pervasive Are Formal Operations? **(p. 522)**? Siegler (1978) and others have shown that adolescents and adults do not always reason in the logical and sophisticated way Piaget described. This can happen when they do not recognize that a particular approach is possible, lack specific knowledge about the task, don't pay attention, lack motivation, or are too overloaded with information to employ complex strategies or solutions. It does seem that individuals with more scholastic ability and achievement are more likely to use formal operational thought in a given situation.

Can Formal Operations Be Taught **(pp. 522-523)**? Piaget felt that formal operations depended upon prior development and thus could not be taught to children who did not have the necessary skills. In fact, both concrete and formal operations have been taught to young children with some degree of success, especially to very intelligent children. Piagetians argue that training studies are artificial and tell us nothing about how the normal process of development unfolds.

Are Formal Operations Related to Academic Performance **(pp. 523-524)**? Performance on formal operational tasks is related to measures of intelligence. Measures of intelligence predict performance in school. Therefore, tests of formal operations can also be used to predict school success. Tests of formal operations predict performance in science and math better than they predict overall academic performance. Explicit training of formal operations has been shown to improve science grades.

III. Other Changes Related to Cognitive Development

A. Adolescent Egocentrism **(pp. 524-525)**

Teenagers often think they are the focus of other people's attention when they are not. This type of egocentrism arises from the newly acquired ability to consider other people's thoughts. Adolescents also have a tendency to think that their thoughts and feelings are unique. That is, having just learned to examine their own thoughts and feelings in a sophisticated way, they do not yet have any reason to believe that others have the same thoughts and feelings. This type of egocentrism declines as peer experience and conversations with friends demonstrate that many adolescents have similar thoughts and feelings.

B. Values and Adolescent Thinking **(pp. 526-527)**

Values are ideas about "good" and "right" behaviors. In adolescence, values become objects of systematic thought and evaluation. One aspect of egocentrism at this age is the adolescent's tendency to overlook the fact that other people have also examined their beliefs in detail. Adolescents often seem idealistic, overconfident, and self-righteous about their beliefs. Instrumental values define proper behavior in seeking goals (for example, honesty, responsibility. Terminal values concern what type of person someone wants to be (for example, happy, safe).

C. The Development of Moral Reasoning **(pp. 527-531)**

Moral judgment, or moral reasoning, is the process of thinking and making decisions about the "proper" thing to do in a particular situation. Both Piaget and Lawrence Kohlberg have provided theories of moral reasoning. According to Piaget, children progress through three perspectives or types of reasoning about right and wrong: amoral reasoning, moral realism, and autonomous morality. Both social and cognitive development influence this progress.

Kohlberg's model of moral reasoning has six distinct stages. He used judgments about hypothetical moral dilemmas to determine the stage at which a person is operating in making decisions about right and wrong. The first two stages are called the preconventional period. The next two stages constitute the period of conventional morality. The last period is called postconventional or principle morality. Kohlberg believed that moral development lags behind cognitive development. Premoral reasoning is typical of children up to 9 years of age. Conventional reasoning is characteristic of most adolescents and adults. Only a few people truly reach the last (highest) stage of moral development.

Criticisms of Kohlberg's theory have focused on measurement problems, the weak relationship between moral judgement and moral behavior, the possibility that types of moral reasoning used are based on the type of moral issue involved, and the possibility that the system is male-biased.

SELF-TEST

Matching: Key Terms and Concepts

G 1.____puberty (p. 503)

E 2.____menarche (p. 504)

I 3.____pituitary gland (p. 505)

P 4.____critical weight (p. 506)

M 5.____hypothetico-deductive reasoning (p. 512)

C 6.____formal operations (p. 513)

J 7.____system of 16 binary operations (p. 520)

B 8.____INRC group (p. 520)

O 9.____cognitive competence (p. 522)

N 10.____cognitive performance (p. 522)

A 11.____imaginary audience (p. 525)

H 12.____moral realism (p. 527)

K 13.____autonomous morality (p. 527)

L 14.____preconventional period (p. 529) obedience punish

F 15.____conventional morality (p. 529) good boy good girl.

D 16.____postconventional period (p. 529) social contract

Look at p 529

a. concern about being the focus of attention

b. four broad logical relationships

c. mental transformations performed in adolescence

d. social contract orientation

e. onset of menstruation

f. good boy/girl orientation

g. entry into adolescence

h. morality is absolute

i. regulates hormonal output of other glands

j. interrelations of factors as in an experiment

k. morality is relative to the situation

l. obedience and punishment orientation

m. cognitive advance during adolescence

n. actual behavior in a particular situation

o. optimal ability

p. theory of the onset of puberty

Multiple Choice Questions

1. The entry into adolescence is called:

   a. menarche
   b. puberty
   c. cognitive competence
   d. moral realism
   (Objective 1, Factual)

2. The gland that has the greatest influence over other glands is the:

   a. pituitary gland
   b. hypothalamus
   c. gonads
   d. neurons
   (Objective 1, Factual)

3. Hormones that travel through the bloodstream and influence the sex glands are called:

   a. gonadotropins
   b. neurons
   c. synapses
   d. hypothalamic releasing factors
   (Objective 1, Factual)

4. Sex glands are referred to as:

   a. synapses
   b. gonadotropins
   c. gonads
   d. neurons
   (Objective 1, Factual)

5. Deep sleep is characterized by:

   a. extremely slow brain waves
   b. the system of 16 binary functions
   c. the INRC group
   d. neurons
   (Objective 1, Factual)

C 6. Brain nerve cells are:

a. the INRC group
b. gonads
c. neurons
d. synapses

(Objective 1, Factual)

D 7. Connections between nerve cells of the brain are called:

a. the system of 16 binary functions
b. the INRC group
c. neurons
d. synapses

(Objective 1, Factual)

C 8. The onset of puberty in boys is marked by:

a. the growing of facial hair
b. the lowering of the voice
c. the ability to ejaculate mobile sperm
d. the increase in height

(Objective 1, Factual)

D 9. Hormone activity in the pituitary is controlled by hormones from the:

a. neurons
b. synapses
c. gonads
d. hypothalamus

(Objective 1, Conceptual)

B 10. The ability to create hypothetical solutions to problems demonstrates:

a. cognitive performance
b. hypothetico-deductive reasoning
c. moral realism
d. autonomous reality

(Objective 2, Factual)

C 11. Adolescents differ from younger children in that:

a. adolescents focus on the concrete
b. children apply logical thinking to possible situations
c. adolescents apply logical thinking to possible situations
d. children use hypothetico-deductive reasoning

(Objective 2, Conceptual)

12. What underlies the cognitive changes that occur in adolescence?

a. moral realism
b. secondary sex characteristics
c. cognitive performance
d. formal operations
(Objective 2, Conceptual)

13. Logical reasoning about abstract concepts occurs in:

a. the preconventional period
b. formal operations
c. preoperational thought
d. concrete operations
(Objective 3, Factual)

14. The ability to consider two variables simultaneously demonstrates:

a. the system of 16 binary operations
b. the INRC group
c. hypothetico-deductive reasoning
d. autonomous reality
(Objective 3, Conceptual)

15. The ability to see reciprocal relationships between variables demonstrates:

a. the INRC group
b. moral realism
c. autonomous morality
d. the system of 16 binary operations
(Objective 3, Conceptual)

16. A typical adolescent's optimal ability is referred to as:

a. moral realism
b. cognitive competence
c. hypothetico-deductive reasoning
d. cognitive performance
(Objective 4, Factual)

17. A typical adolescent's actual behavior on a particular task is:

a. moral realism
b. cognitive competence
c. cognitive performance
d. hypothetico-deductive reasoning
(Objective 4, Factual)

D 18. Which of the following is illustrated by a teenager's belief that he or she is the focus of other people's attention?

a. moral realism
b. cognitive competence
c. personal fable
d. egocentrism — imaginary audience
(Objective 5, Factual)

B 19. A teenager's belief that his or her thoughts and feelings are unique is called:

a. menarche
b. a personal fable
c. imaginary audience
d. moral realism
(Objective 5, Factual)

A 20. Morality viewed as an absolute is characteristic of:

a. moral realism
b. autonomous morality
c. cognitive competence
d. postconventional morality
(Objective 6, Conceptual)

D 21. Considering situational aspects of moral dilemmas is characteristic of:

a. postconventional morality
b. personal fable
c. moral realism
d. autonomous morality
(Objective 6, Conceptual)

C 22. Judgments based on obedience and punishment are characteristic of:

a. the postconventional period
b. autonomous morality
c. the preconventional period
d. the conventional period
(Objective 7, Conceptual)

look up p. 329

A 23. Judgments based on internalized standards are characteristic of:

a. the conventional period
b. the hypothetico-deductive reasoning
c. the postconventional period
d. the preconventional period
(Objective 7, Conceptual)

24. Judgments that use the criterion of social contract concepts are characteristic of:

a. the conventional period
b. moral realism
c. the preconventional period
d. the postconventional period

(Objective 7, Conceptual)

ESSAY QUESTIONS

1. Summarize the major cognitive advances made in adolescence.

2. Summarize Kohlberg's theory of moral development.

VIGNETTE HIGHLIGHT

Multiple Choice Questions

B 1. Meryl says, "Sometimes my Mom is so dense. She just doesn't understand what it's like to be my age." This is an example of:

a. egocentrism
b. personal fable
c. imaginary audience
d. moral realism

C 2. Mikey Gordon systematically questions his mother about her car trouble. This is an example of:

a. cognitive performance
b. autonomous reality
c. hypothetico-deductive reasoning
d. moral realism

C 3. At a community action meeting, Malcolm argues that it is unfair to place low income housing away from the middle of the neighborhood, where it would be far from shopping. What period of moral development is this type of reasoning typical of?

a. preconventional period
b. conventional period
c. postconventional period
d. moral realism

Essay Questions

1. As Malcolm reaches middle adolescence, he seems quite ready to develop interests and responsibilities beyond the family. He wants to take a job as a stock clerk and is making plans for dating and other aspects of a typical teenage social life. Discuss some aspects of his family life that might make a difference between good and bad outcomes as Malcolm becomes more independent of his family.

2. As an adolescent, Meryl is beginning to see her mother as an obstacle to many of her activities. Discuss cognitive factors that might account for some of this attitude.

ANSWER KEYS

Matching

1. g 2. e 3. i 4. p 5. m 6. c 7. j 8. b

9. o 10. n 11. a 12. h 13. k 14. l 15. f 16. d

Multiple Choice

1. b (p. 503)	13. b (p. 513)
2. a (p. 505)	14. a (p. 520)
3. a (p. 505)	15. a (p. 521)
4. c (p. 505)	16. b (p. 522)
5. a (p. 510)	17. c (p. 522)
6. c (p. 510)	18. d (p. 525)
7. d (p. 510)	19. b (p. 525)
8. c (p. 504)	20. a (p. 527)
9. d (p. 505)	21. d (p. 527)
10. b (p. 512)	22. c (p. 529)
11. c (p. 512)	23. a (p. 529)
12. d (p. 513)	24. d (p. 529)

Essay Questions

1. There are a number of cognitive advances in adolescence. First, logical thinking is now applied to hypothetical objects or situations. Earlier, logical thought was only applied to real, concrete objects and situations. A related development is hypothetico-deductive reasoning. This is the ability to consider hypothetical solutions to a problem and then formulate a logical and systematic approach for deducing which solution is correct. Third, adolescents can think about relationships among mentally constructed, or abstract, concepts. These changes result in a variety of changes in social reasoning. Adolescents apply their new ability to think about their own ideas and feelings to personally and socially significant issues. They often become interested in philosophy, politics, and religion. They often display very egocentric confidence in their conclusions about these topics and lack of respect for the depth of other people's thinking. They also tend to think that many of their thoughts and feelings are unique. They eventually discover that other adolescents have similar thoughts and feelings **(pp. 512-513).**

2. Kohlberg identified six stages of moral development which are broken up into three periods. The first period is called the preconventional period and consists of the hedonistic and instrumental stages. The second period is called conventional morality. In this period there are also two stages, one representing a good boy or good girl orientation, and the other focusing on a person's duty to conform to society's laws and rules. The last period is called the postconventional period or principle morality. This period consists of a social contract orientation in stage 5 and the hierarchy of principles orientation in stage 6. Kohlberg felt that moral judgment followed cognitive development and depended upon it. Critics have argued that people who show reasoning typical of one stage when faced with one problem may use reasoning typical of another stage when faced with a different problem. Thus moral judgment may be less a stage or trait of the person than Kohlberg thought **(pp. 528-529).**

VIGNETTE ANSWER KEYS

Multiple Choice

1. b (p. 525)   2. c (p. 512)   3. c (p. 529)

Essay Questions

1. As Malcolm becomes independent he could go on to make his mark as a person and community leader, or he could fall in with delinquent models that are readily available to him. The two most obvious factors in his family life that seem likely to point him toward a good outcome involve models and parental control. His parents' behavior as individuals and the good quality of their relationship provide models that Malcolm can both imitate and think about. As an adolescent he can now think about the challenges his parents faced and about the many different facets of their behavior. He can also think about situations he might fall into and consider the consequences without actually having to suffer them. He can consider what his parents have done, and might have done, and also how situations he meets are similar to and different from situations they faced. Malcolm's family also seems to be putting him on the right track by encouraging his independence, rather than pushing it or resisting it. This is especially clear in the way they make him keep up his household duties along with taking a job. This makes the point that they are still exercising supervision, that independence means more work, not less, and that independence will be limited if he abuses it.

2. As Meryl enters adolescence she is acquiring the ability to think about feelings and emotions, to consider hypothetical situations and events, and to see relationships among complex ideas and concepts. She is beginning to notice things in her mother's behavior that didn't seem to be there before. In particular, her mother seems to be becoming a pain and an obstacle. Although Meryl sees this as change in her mother, it is likely that much of what she sees is due to changes in her. First of all, as her cognitive abilities expand, she begins to see possibilities that didn't seem to be there before. Unfortunately, she doesn't have much experience with many of these new activities yet, and so she underestimates problems and consequences that her mother can see very clearly. Some of the limits her mother places on her are limits she might place on herself if she had experience to go with her new cognitive abilities. Meryl's new view of the world also leads to plans and behavior that cause her mother to change. That is, her mother is not placing new restrictions on Meryl because of a new tendency toward restrictiveness. In large part the increased restrictions are following Meryl's new plans and behavior. Finally, much of what Meryl is feeling as problem behavior by her mother is likely to be the same behavior her mother has exhibited for years in one form or another. But as an adolescent, Meryl can think about this behavior in new ways now. She sees restrictions that she didn't realize before and she also starts looking at her mother's behavior in terms of fairness and social norms. This is new too.

Chapter 15
Social Development in Adolescence

Learning Objectives

When you have studied the material in this chapter, you will be able to:

1. Explain why adolescence is a stormy period in social development, and explain the difference between early and late adolescence.
2. Describe the possible routes of identity formation for teenagers.
3. Describe the developmental processes involved in establishing an integrated self-concept.
4. Explain the social construction view of identity formation and discuss the importance of family influence during adolescence.
5. Describe the characteristics of friendship and peer group membership during adolescence.
6. Describe the challenge that adolescents have to deal with in school and working environments.
7. Discuss the three most severe problems of teenagers in Western culture: teenage pregnancy, alcohol and drug use, and running away.

CHAPTER SUMMARY

I. The Social World of Adolescence: An Overview

A. How Stormy Is Adolescence **(pp. 536-538)?**

The notion that adolescence is a stormy period in development is too simple. The types and amount of disruption are different for different individuals and in different situations. Teenagers encounter more stress between ages 13 and 16 than at other periods in adolescence. Teenagers tend to argue with parents on issues of homework, house chores, mannerisms, hair styles and clothing. But most of them have similar values and beliefs to those of their parents. Psychologists have distinguished between patterns of tumultuous growth, surgent growth, and continuous growth. Different children follow different patterns through adolescence. When adolescents are in conflict with parents it is more often a matter of increasing self-assertion than of true rebellion or defiance.

B. A Cross-Cultural Perspective **(pp.538-539)**

Adolescence seems less stressful in cultures in which there is an agreed-upon age for becoming an adult and a set of rituals (puberty rites or rites of passage) that mark entry into adulthood. Western cultures also tend to delay the transition to adulthood, in part because of the time required for education. Vagueness about when a child becomes "adult", the frustration of prolonged striving for autonomy, and the delay of full entry into adult sexual role impose special challenges on both adolescents and their parents in Western cultures.

C. The Tasks of Adolescence **(pp. 539-540)**

The key tasks of social development in adolescence are:

1. Establish a personal identity.
2. Achieve a new level of peer relations.
3. Acquire a more equal, independent, and responsible status in the family.
4. Move toward a more autonomous stance with respect to personal choices and values.

II. Development of the Self

A. Progress Toward Identity **(pp. 540-543)**

The Concept of a Personal Identity **(p. 541).** Erikson described identity as a quest for personal discovery, and a growing understanding of the meaning of "who I am." Rapid development of sexual urges, cognitive abilities, and family demands for responsibility demand rapid changes in the adolescent's self-concept.

Individual Differences in Identity Formation **(pp. 541-543).** Interview studies with adolescents suggest that there are different routes to establishing personal identity at this age. These include foreclosure, identity diffusion, moratorium, and identity achievement. According to Erikson, basic trust and autonomy acquired early in childhood, and the sense of confidence and mastery developed in middle childhood, can help a child meet the challenges of adolescent identity formation.

B. Changes in Self-Concept Across the Teenage Years **(pp. 543-547)**

The Declining Fragility of the Self **(p. 544).** Through interaction with others and school achievement, young teens gradually become realistic and confident in their self-appraisals. The self-concept becomes more stable across time. They become more willing to disclose their ideas and personal thoughts to others.

Other Changes in Self-Concept **(pp. 544-545).** Adolescents' self-concepts change in many dimensions. Differentiation, individuation, increased psychological orientation, and self-reflection are among the most important areas of change. These changes lead to a more coherent system of values and behavior toward the end of adolescence.

Evidence for Two Adolescent Subphases **(pp. 545-547).** Older adolescents (ages 17 to 18) have a more sophisticated self-understanding than do young adolescents (ages 13 to 15). Older adolescents can understand the difference between a "real" and a "phony" self. They have a more integrated knowledge of how different aspects of the self are tied together into a whole. And the sense of being the focus of other people's attention declines.

III. Peer Relations in Adolescence

A. Advances in Understanding Others **(pp. 547-549)**

Along with advances in self-awareness, adolescents are able to grasp other people's thoughts and feelings according to their understanding of themselves.

B. Changes in the Nature of Friendship **(pp. 549-552)**

The capacity for mutual understanding between friends increases in adolescence. Friendship begins to imply loyalty and willingness to keep personal secrets. As they grow older, adolescents are able to have a wider range of different friends, with whom they do different things. Friendships become more likely to last over many years and more like those found in adulthood. Both Erikson and Sullivan stressed the relation between intimacy among peers and personal identity.

C. Peer Groups in Adolescence **(pp. 552-554)**

Cliques are characterized by the close-knit intimate fellowship among the members. A girls' clique is often closed to newcomers. A crowd is larger, less exclusive, and more loosely organized than a clique. A crowd offers a broader range of informal contacts for teenagers. There are four stages in the emergence and development of adolescent peer groups. Each stage involves different patterns of clique and crowd behavior.

D. Dating and Sexual Activity **(p. 554)**

By age 16, 90 percent of youngsters are dating. Sexual experimentation usually does not begin until mid-adolescence. Most teenagers value exclusivity and fidelity between sexual partners.

E. The Relative Influence of Peers **(pp. 554-556)**

The process of identifying with peers helps youngsters to de-identity with parents and affirm their uniqueness. There are individual and situational differences in terms of peer group conformity: (1) Middle-status peers are more likely to conform than high- or low-status peers. (2) Friends are more influential than acquaintances. (3) Teenage friends have their greatest effect on superficial behaviors. Adolescents tend to follow their parents in many basic philosophies and attitudes.

IV. Family Relations in Adolescence

A. The Changing Family Structure **(pp. 557-560)**

Cognitive development allows adolescents to see imperfections in parental behaviors, seek greater autonomy in behavior and decision making, and look for new ways to relate to parents. Family conflict and parental stress usually peak at age 14 to 15, then decrease. During this period, healthy families are as likely to experience conflicts as unhealthy families. Conflicts are often the first step toward a more balanced family structure.

B. Parenting Patterns and Adolescent Development **(pp. 560-562)**

The most successful parents of adolescents are those who stay involved, offer guidance and feedback instead of demands and directives, and allow their children to become full partners in the family.

C. Bi-Directional Influence **(p. 562)**

A child's behavior during adolescence clearly influences parental behavior. Parents tend to allow their sons greater freedom to be away from home, and have more concern about their daughters' sexual behavior.

D. The Impact of Divorce on Adolescents **(pp. 562-563)**

The effects of divorce may not appear until years later, especially in girls. It also appears that the effects of divorce are due to more than just separation from one of the parents or living in a single-parent family.

V. Adolescents in the Broader World

A. Adolescents at School **(pp. 564-566)**

School can have many good influences on teenagers. Unfortunately, it often demands too much conformity and rewards popularity and athletic performance more than scholastic achievement. In this society, academic achievement has some validity as an index of good social adjustment. Adolescents' learning motivations are influenced largely by (1) parental attitudes and modeling, and (2) locus of control.

B. Adolescents at Work **(p. 566)**

Job experience can allow adolescents to feel competent, anticipate future roles, learn responsibility, and practice managing money. Unfortunately, the types of jobs most available to adolescents are routine and impersonal. They can lead to a sense of working for money and little more. Combining work and school can reduce both schoolwork and peer experience.

C. Adolescents and Career Development **(p. 566-567)**

Orientation toward work and toward particular types of career interests often begins to develop in the teen years. Since teens lack wide experience with different types of occupations, help from school counselors and parents can be helpful.

VI. Common Problems of Adolescence

Experimentation with drugs and sexuality is common, even among well adjusted adolescents. However, drug abuse, teenage pregnancy and runaway youths are nationwide problems and predict later difficulties in adulthood.

A. Alcohol and Drug Use **(pp. 567-568)**

The most popular mind-altering drug among adolescents is alcohol, the second is marijuana. Teenagers consume alcohol or drugs because (1) their friends do so, (2) they can feel as if they are no longer children and try to behave as they think adults do, and (3) they want to have fun and ease tensions in social situations. Intensive drug use may (1) constrict mutual exploration among peers that is necessary for identity achievement, (2) prevent the development of effective coping skills, and (3) lead to or amplify psychological problems.

B. Teenage Pregnancy **(pp. 568-569)**

Teenage girls become pregnant because (1) most of them remain unaware of the high risk period for conception, (2) they feel it is wrong to plan to have sex and therefore do not use contraception during their first sexual experiences, (3) they are convinced that they won't be the one to get pregnant, and (4) parents fail to monitor the their dating. Teenage pregnancy can (1) curtail the mother's education and career, (2) lead to poor parenting by girls ill-prepared for motherhood, and (3) trap the mother and child in a cycle of poverty.

C. Running Away **(pp. 569-570)**

If teenagers cannot receive enough support at home, they may express their autonomy by the extreme action of running away. Each year hundred of thousands of young teenagers run away from home for such reasons or, in more extreme cases, because of physical or sexual abuse. In late adolescence, running away usually takes the form of joining religious cults. Cults demand total commitment and thus may tap the feeling of loneliness and idealism which is the most vulnerable part of older adolescents.

SELF-TEST

Matching: Key Terms and Concepts

1. ____ tumultuous growth (p. 537)
2. ____ surgent growth (p. 537)
3. ____ continuous growth (p. 537)
4. ____ puberty rites (p. 539)
5. ____ identity crisis (p. 541)
6. ____ foreclosure (p. 541)
7. ____ identity diffusion (p. 542)
8. ____ moratorium (p. 542)
9. ____ identity achievement (p. 542)
10. ____ (personal) identity (p. 543)
11. ____ personal fable (p. 544)
12. ____ intimacy (p. 551)
13. ____ clique (p. 552)
14. ____ crowd (p. 552)
15. ____ social construction view (of identity formation) (p. 556)

a. no struggle for identity formation

b. importance of supportive relationship

c. reasonable adjustment of teenage boys

d. retreat, then consolidate the identity

e. emotional aspects of a friendship

f. patchwork self

g. sense of self-assurance of teenage boys

h. belief of invulnerability

i. ultimate identity formation

j. conflicts of teenage boys

k. a large peer group

l. rites of passage

m. an integrated, coherent, and goal-directed self

n. teenager identity

o. close friends

Multiple Choice Questions

A 1. The "stormy period" of adolescence usually appears:

a. in the early teenage years (ages 13 to 16)
b. in the late teenage years (ages 16-18)
c. all through the teenage years
d. right before the teenage years
(Objective 1, Factual)

A 2. Which girls are more likely to be dissatisfied with themselves and their bodies? Those who mature:

a. early
b. late
c. both a and b
d. none of the above
(Objective 1, Factual)

B 3. Which boys are most likely to experience problems with parents and peers? Those who mature:

a. early
b. late
c. both a and b
d. none of the above
(Objective 1, Factual)

A 4. Margaret Mead found that Samoan adolescents:

a. enter adulthood early and gradually
b. enter adulthood late and gradually
c. enter adulthood after they have their "puberty rites"
d. can anticipate exactly when they are going to become adults
(Objective 1, Factual)

D 5. Who first used the term identity crisis?

a. Freud
b. Mead
c. Selman
d. Erikson
(Objective 2, Factual)

D 6. Teenagers who are obedient to authority have adopted the identity formation known as:

a. moratorium
b. identity achievement
c. identity diffusion
d. foreclosure
(Objective 2, Factual)

D 7. Which of the following places the categories of identity formation in order, from healthiest to least healthy?

a. moratorium, identity achievement, identity diffusion, and foreclosure
b. foreclosure, identity achievement, moratorium, and identity diffusion
c. identity achievement, foreclosure, moratorium, and identity diffusion
d. identity achievement, moratorium, foreclosure, and identity diffusion
(Objective 2, Conceptual)

C B 8. The belief that others are scrutinizing the self peaks at about the age of:

a. 10
b. 12
c. 14
d. 16
(Objective 3, Factual)

C 9. The distorted belief that "No harm can befall me" is called:

a. imaginary audience
b. self-reflection
c. personal fable
d. self-watching
(Objective 3, Conceptual)

C 10. During adolescence, self-concept becomes more oriented toward:

a. athletic ability
b. age
c. psychological and personality characteristics
d. similarity to parents
(Objective 3, Conceptual)

A 11. How does the sense of being the center of other peoples' attention change during adolescence?

a. decreases
b. increases
c. stays the same
d. decreases, then increases
(Objective 3, Conceptual)

B 12. Where is parental influence strongest on teens?

a. hair style and clothing
b. basic values and philosophy
c. doing house chores
d. choice of friends
(Objective 4, Factual)

B 13. What age child is likely to be most difficult for a parent experiencing a "midlife crisis"?

a. toddler
b. early teen
c. late teen
d. young, independent adult
(Objective 4, Factual)

D 14. Which of the following statements about teenage girls is <u>not</u> true?

a. They are more self-consciousness than teenage boys.
b. They have lower self-esteem than teenage boys.
c. Adolescent conflict lasts longer than for boys.
d. Their conflicts involve escaping the confines of the family.
(Objective 4, Factual)

C 15. Which of the following indicates that the effects of divorce are <u>not</u> simply due to single parenting or loss of a parent?

a. The effects on boys and girls are different.
b. The effects of father custody and mother custody are different.
c. The effects of divorce and death of one parent are different.
d. The effects depend on the age of the child.
(Objective 4, Factual)

C 16. When does the capacity for intimacy with peers typically emerge?

a. late in middle childhood
b. early adolescence
c. late adolescence
d. young adulthood
(Objective 5, Factual)

D 17. The fact that teenagers spend hours talking with one another shows a strong desire for:

a. self-reflection
b. self constancy
c. self-esteem
d. self-disclosure
(Objective 5, Conceptual)

C 18. The emotional aspect of friendship is usually called:

a. mutual understanding
b. self-disclosure
c. intimacy
d. fidelity
(Objective 5, Conceptual)

D 19. What roles do cliques and crowds play in teen peer relations?

a. Cliques are more important.
b. Crowds are more important.
c. Cliques are same-sex, crowds are mixed-sex.
d. They play different but important roles.
(Objective 5, Conceptual)

A 20. How do clique relationships change over the teen years?

a. change from same-sex to mixed-sex
b. give way to crowd membership
c. tend to be stable over the teen years
d. all of the above
(Objective 5, Conceptual)

D 21. Which of the following is the earliest stage of teen peer relationships?

a. Male and female unisex cliques begin to interact.
b. Several heterosexual cliques interact.
c. Some upper-status members of the crowd form a heterosexual clique.
d. Teenagers participate only in unisex cliques.
(Objective 5, Conceptual)

D 22. Which of the following statements about sources of academic motivation in girls is false?

a. Parents tend to see math talent in boys rather than girls.
b. Success does not give girls as much pride as it does boys.
c. Girls often assign negative social value to math achievement.
d. Girls are often socialized to feel instrumental competence.
(Objective 6, Factual)

D 23. Which of the following is (are) related to the causes of teen pregnancy?

a. feeling that it is wrong to plan to have sex
b. parents fail to monitor girls' dating habits
c. ignorance about birth control
d. all of the above
(Objective 7, Factual)

A 24. Some children join religious cults and run away from home. These children are usually:

a. older adolescents
b. younger adolescents
c. older school age children
d. younger school age children

(Objective 7, Conceptual)

ESSAY QUESTIONS

1. Anthropologists found that the transition to adulthood for teenagers in certain tribes is not as difficult as the transition to adulthood in modern Western society. Explain why young people in this society so easily become "lost" when they reach adolescence.

adult status withheld

but some responsibility given

2. Explain the social construction view of identity formation proposed by James Youniss (1983).

supportive relationships with others (parents) help form persons identity

understanding ones own unique perspective and how it relates to the perspectives of others.

VIGNETTE HIGHLIGHT

Multiple Choice Questions

B 1. That Meryl and Amy would lock themselves in a room talking for hours illustrates the need for ____________.

a. identity formation
b. self-disclosure
c. self-reflectiveness
d. social comparison

A 2. For a period of time, Meryl viewed her mother as an obstacle blocking all the things that Meryl wanted to do. This stormy feeling is actually quite common when the child is:

a. in early adolescence
b. in the transition from early to late adolescence
c. in late adolescence
d. in the transition from late adolescence to early adulthood

B 3. Meryl had attend many mixed-sex parties, but she had never gone out on a date before. Which stage of peer relations is this?

a. unisex cliques
b. beginning of the crowd
c. crowd in transition
d. crowd disintegration

Essay Questions

1. Malcolm never seems to have come very close to falling in with delinquent peers. Suggest two things that his family did, other than supervise him closely, that may have made him more likely to have reasonable friends and interests rather than delinquent ones.

Modeled good behavior.

accepted him so he had good self concept.

2. Mikey Gordon took a marked turn for the better in his high school years. Suggest two sources of this important change.

teacher & uncle who took an interest in him.

ANSWER KEYS

Matching

1. j 2. c 3. g 4. l 5. n 6. a 7. f 8. d 9. i

10. m 11. h 12. e 13. o 14. k 15. b

Multiple Choice

1. a (p. 537)
2. b (p. 537)
3. a (p. 537)
4. a (pp. 538-539)
5. d (p. 541)
6. d (p. 543)
7. d (pp. 541-542)
8. c (p. 547)
9. c (p. 544)
10. c (pp. 544-545)
11. a (p. 555)
12. b (p. 537)
13. b (p. 557)
14. d (p. 562)
15. c (pp. 562-563)
16. c (p. 554)
17. d (p. 550)
18. c (p. 551)
19. d (p. 552)
20. a (p. 552)
21. d (p. 553)
22. d (p. 565)
23. d (p. 569)
24. a (p. 570)

Essay Questions

1. Transition into adulthood occurs later in Western cultures than in many others. Part of the explanation for this seems to be that more industrialized cultures require that one have greater education and experience before participating in the types of work necessary to support an independent household. Thus one of the reasons Western adolescents often get "lost" in the teen years is that this difficult period is prolonged. In addition, the demands of employment and family responsibilities are not there to provide clear goals and exposure to models **(pp. 538-539).**

2. The central point in Youniss's social construction view of identity formation is that identity formation is not something a person achieves by going off and thinking about it. To achieve an identity involves understanding one's own unique perspective as well as how it relates to the perspectives of others. This can be accomplished only through social interaction. A mutually supportive parent-child relationship can help both parents and adolescents in practicing their newly evolving roles. The mutual criticism can help clarify and confirm the adolescents' self-assertiveness and the parents' mix of accepting and challenging this new status. Peer relationships also play an important role in identity formation **(pp. 556-557).**

VIGNETTE ANSWER KEYS

Multiple Choice

1. b **(p. 550)** 2. a **(p. 537)** 3. b **(p. 552)**

Essay Questions

1. John and DeeDee gave Malcolm a clear set of prosocial beliefs, including the expectation that Malcolm would go to college. In addition, they gave him clear training and experience in taking responsibility for his own behavior.

   Malcolm's father successfully channeled Malcolm's idealism toward something positive and practical. Remember that Malcolm in middle childhood had some uncomfortable experience with "white children." The hatred could have simmered in his mind, increased and finally led to antisocial rather than prosocial expressions.

2. Two of the most obvious influences were people he met outside his immediate family. First, the biology teacher seemed to turn Mikey's life around by interesting him in biology and providing a model for later schooling. Although there was an element of luck in this, it was clearly much more likely to happen if he were in school than if he had dropped out. This emphasizes an important point. School is not just a place to learn classwork. It is also a place to encounter positive models for interests and roles that might never be encountered in the family or neighborhood. So in some cases, more time in school can be good in and of itself.

   Second, Uncle Dan's encouragement confirmed Mikey's interest in biology. His father never favored academic interests, and after his parents' divorce he had become withdrawn and depressed. Since his relationships to both his mother and his father were not close, Mikey might have failed to carry through on his new interest in school and college if he had not had someone like Dan to confide in and to encourage him. It is possible, after all, for the family side of a child's life to cancel out positive things from other sources. Dan helped Mikey firm up his new self-image and gave practical advice as well. Mikey might not have gotten this at school, even from Mr. Rosengren, simply because of the large number of students each teacher is responsible for.

Chapter 16
Developmental Psychopathology

LEARNING OBJECTIVES

When you have studied the material in this chapter, you will be able to:

1. Define the concept of developmental psychopathology and name the main factors studied as the causes of psychological problems.
2. Name and describe the main biological models of developmental psychopathology.
3. Name and describe the main environmental models of developmental psychopathology.
4. Define the developmental perspective in the study of developmental psychopathology.
5. Describe the main characteristics of early childhood autism.
6. Describe the main characteristics of hyperactivity or attention deficit disorder.
7. Describe the main characteristics of conduct disorders.
8. Describe the main characteristics of anxiety disorders.
9. Describe the main characteristics of anorexia nervosa.
10. Describe the main characteristics of depression.

CHAPTER SUMMARY

I. Models of Psychopathology

(Pp. 580-581) Models or views of psychopathology differ in the emphasis they place on biological and environmental factors as causes of psychological disorders.

A. Biological Perspectives **(pp. 581-584)**

The Traditional Medical Model **(p. 581).** The model assumes that psychological problems have an underlying biological cause. Emotional and behavioral problems are viewed as symptoms of structural or physiological malfunction of the body, typically of the brain. Some mental disorders of childhood seem to fit the medical model. Others clearly do not.

Modern Neurological and Physiological Models **(pp. 581-582).** These models suggest that chemical imbalances in the brain are the cause of psychological disorders. These ideas are too new for us to have evaluated their relevance to many psychological problems.

Genetic Models **(pp. 582-584).** Genetic models suggest that some people inherit a predisposition to develop emotional and behavioral problems. In some cases, the genetic basis for a physiological or neurological problem may involve more than one gene. Twin studies provide evidence for a hereditary factor in schizophrenia, but there is also evidence for a substantial influence of environmental factors. The diathesis/stress model sees schizophrenia as a product of contributions made by both hereditary and environmental factors.

B. Environmental Perspectives **(pp. 584-588)**

Sociological Models **(p. 584).** Sociological models emphasize the social context surrounding individuals with psychological problems. Many different psychological problems have been dealt with from a sociological perspective.

Behavioral Models **(pp. 584-586).** Behavioral models emphasize environmental factors too. But the emphasis is on the rewards, punishments, and modeled behaviors provided to the child, rather than on social and family structure per se. Recent cognitive-behavioral models include internal cognitive processes among the things that can be mislearned and treated with behavior modification methods.

Psychodynamic Models **(p. 586).** Psychodynamic models assume an underlying emotional cause for any psychological problem. Accordingly, psychodynamic therapists do not think it is enough to treat the behavioral symptoms of the problem.

Family Models (pp. 586-588). Family models assume that while one person in the family is usually identified as disturbed, in actuality that person's symptoms are a reflection of disturbance in the family system. It is the system, not the individual, that is disturbed. Family models have something in common with psychodynamic models in that they search for deeper meanings behind a person's behaviors.

C. The Developmental Perspective **(pp. 590-592)**

The developmental perspective draws upon each of the models described. It also assumes that it is essential to think of both the origin and the cure of childhood problems in a framework that takes the child's age and abilities, and the course of development, into account.

II. Some Childhood Disorders

A. Early Childhood Autism **(pp. 590-592)**

The main characteristics of autism are a powerful insistence on preserving sameness in the environment, extreme social isolation, and severe speech deficits, including muteness and echoing. Autistic children have great trouble learning simple abstract concepts, although they seem to have normal memory for routinized information. Autistic children have physically normal appearance and usually they do not have obvious brain damage. Most researchers agree that some as yet unidentified organic disorder must be involved.

B. Hyperactivity or Attention Deficit Disorder **(pp.592-595)**

Hyperactive children do not represent a single type. The term hyperactive is restricted to children with normal intelligence and no neurological handicaps. Hyperactivity is more common in boys and first-borns.

Causes of Hyperactivity **(pp. 593-594)**. Most theories of hyperactivity have emphasized biological factors and therapy based on medication. Behaviorally oriented theories and therapies have also been influential. An approach focusing on intrusive, seductive, or overstimulating styles of parenting has also received some recent support. It may be that different cases have different causes or that several causes are involved in some cases.

Treatment and Prognosis **(pp. 594-595)**. Stimulant drugs (most often Ritalin), are frequently used to treat hyperactivity. A review of the evidence shows (1) the stimulants work because they enhance the abilities to concentrate, sustain attention, and persist at routine tasks, there is nothing paradoxical about the effects of stimulants; (2) that stimulants can improve the performance of hyperactive children does not indicate a biochemical need for them; (3) there is reason to be concerned about the long-term effects of stimulants. Behavioral therapies offer an alternative to drug therapy. Behavioral therapies with medication are more effective than medication alone. Without therapy, many hyperactive children continue to have problems through adolescence.

C. Conduct Disorders (pp. 596-598)

A conduct disorder is a persistent pattern of behavior in which the child repeatedly violates either the basic rights of others or age-appropriate social norms. Aggression and antisocial behavior are quite stable during childhood years. They are also very strong predictors of similar problems in adulthood. Factors such as low intelligence, size, strength, gender, and hormonal influences may contribute to conduct disorders. But environmental factors are also very important. Many studies have found links between conduct disorders and family variables such as marital discord, hostility, unavailability, rejection, and child abuse.

D. Anxiety Disorders (pp. 599-600)

Childhood anxiety disorders are less frequent than conduct disorders, and they are more likely to go away without professional help. Anxiety disorders are generally not predictive of serious problems in adulthood. The evidence gathered so far seems to indicate that family factors are the principal causes.

E. Anorexia Nervosa (pp. 600-602)

Anorexia nervosa is primarily a problem of adolescent and young adult women, and is more common in the middle class. Psychological theories that focus on the family seem more promising. Women are exposed to a great deal of social pressure related to food, fitness, and beauty. This may be a factor in the development of anorexia nervosa and in the fact that it is so difficult to treat. There is some evidence of short-term success of behavioral therapies. There is also evidence that family therapy may have longer-term success.

F. Depression (pp. 602-604)

Depressed adolescents are inactive and unmotivated. They may refuse food and have thoughts of suicide. Depressed children and adolescents tend to blame themselves and feel powerless. There is little clear evidence that biological factors are major explanations of childhood depression. Bowlby suggests that depression can be initiated by a series of early losses, or by a major loss in the context of inadequate care, which leads to inadequate mourning. An alternative perspective is that loss of a parent, negative conditions, and learned helplessness are the common factors underlying depression. Other psychological theories center on severe emotional neglect by parents.

SELF-TEST

Matching: Key Terms and Concepts

1.___ etiology (p. 580)
2.___ medical model (p. 581)
3.___ diathesis/stress model (p. 583)
4.___ Amish (p. 583)
5.___ behavioral model (p. 584)
6.___ generalization (p. 585)
7.___ autism (p. 590)
8.___ echolalia (p. 591)
9.___ attention deficit (p. 593)
10.___ conduct disorder (p. 596)
11.___ anxiety disorder (p. 599)
12.___ spontaneous remission (p. 600)
13.___ anorexia nervosa (p. 600)
14.___ bulimia (p. 601)
15.___ depression (p. 602)

a. symptoms are the problem
b. eating disorder
c. hyperactive disorder
d. extreme social isolation
e. study of causes
f. induction of vomiting
g. separation disorder
h. "gene for depression"
i. perspective on schizophrenia
j. frequent thoughts of suicide
k. failure to develop normal bonds
l. carrying over to other situations
m. symptoms/physical cause
n. lifeless repetition of a sound
o. recovery without therapy

Multiple Choice Questions

C 1. A developmental approach to psychopathology:

   a. emphasizes a child's genetic vulnerability
   b. emphasizes risks in a child's environment
   c. studies the developmental roots of adult disorders
   d. none of the above

   (Objective 1, Factual)

A 2. A model of psychopathology is:

   a. a set of ideas about the causes of psychological problems
   b. a subfield of developmental psychology
   c. the study of contrasting patterns of adaptation over time
   d. etiology

   (Objective 1, Conceptual)

B 3. The traditional medical model assumes that whenever a psychological problem arises, it has causes that are:

   a. environmental
   b. biological
   c. interactional
   d. none of the above

   (Objective 2, Conceptual)

C 4. The neurological and physiological models suggest that the cause of psychological problems is:

   a. structural brain damage
   b. certain genes
   c. chemical imbalances in the brain
   d. all of the above

   (Objective 2, Factual)

B 5. Which of the following assumes that predisposition to develop emotional and behavioral problems is inherited?

   a. sociological models
   b. genetic models
   c. neurological and physiological models
   d. traditional medical models

   (Objective 2, Conceptual)

A 6. Which of the following models would examine a case of child delinquency in terms of the type of neighborhood the child lived in?

a. sociological models
b. behavioral models
c. psychodynamic models
d. family models
(Objective 3, Conceptual)

D 7. Recent behavioral models take into account internal cognitive processes. This reflects difficulties strictly behavioral therapy was having with:

a. expectations and beliefs of troubled patients
b. the successful treatment of psychological disorders
c. the behavioral model that emphasizes rewards and punishments
d. the generalization of results to other settings
(Objective 3, Factual)

D 8. Psychodynamic models assume that:

a. disturbed behavior is the problem to be treated
b. disturbed behavior is the manifestation of a physical cause
c. symptoms are secondary causes of problems
d. disturbed behavior is the manifestation of thoughts and feelings produced by life experiences
(Objective 3, Conceptual)

C 9. Which of the following approaches would look at relationships between a child's parents and siblings in order to understand a behavior problem occurring at school?

a. psychodynamic
b. behavioral
c. family
d. developmental
(Objective 3, Conceptual)

D 10. The developmental perspective considers:

a. biological and cultural factors
b. reinforcing and punishment experiences
c. family relationships and behavioral adaptations over time
d. all of the above
(Objective 4, Factual)

A 11. Repetitive body rocking and flicking of the fingers engaged in by autistic children may reflect:

a. insistence on preserving sameness in the environment
b. extreme social isolation
c. severe speech deficits
d. difficulty modulating sensory input
(Objective 5, Factual)

B 12. Which of the following is a language deficit in autism?

a. avoiding personal interactions
b. echolalia
c. autistic aloneness
d. maintaining the sameness of the environment
(Objective 5, Conceptual)

D 13. Researchers agree that some form of organic disorder must be involved in autism because studies have shown that:

a. siblings of autistic children are usually normal
b. profound language and cognitive deficits persist after treatment
c. autism is statistically related to certain biological problems
d. all of the above
(Objective 5, Factual)

C 14. Hyperactive children generally:

a. present neurological handicaps
b. have less than normal intelligence
c. have attention-related difficulties
d. all of the above
(Objective 6, Factual)

A 15. Which theories of hyperactivity have predominated despite questionable supportive evidence?

a. organic theories
b. parenting style perspectives
c. family theories
d. environmental perspectives
(Objective 6, Factual)

D 16. The theory of the paradoxical drug effect is flawed because:

a. effects are the same in both hyperactive and normal children
b. drug effectiveness does not prove biochemical causes
c. there are doubts about the long-term effects of drugs
d. all of the above
(Objective 6, Factual)

B 17. Helen is a 7-year-old child who disobeys her teachers and is very violent with her classmates. She would fall into the category of:

a. hyperactivity disorders
b. conduct disorders
c. anxiety disorders
d. depressive disorders
(Objective 7, Conceptual)

A 18. What is the most likely explanation for conduct disorder?

a. parental marital discord, hostility, and unavailability
b. threshold of nervous system arousal and low intelligence
c. hormonal levels and low intelligence
d. gender, strength, hormonal levels, and low intelligence
(Objective 7, Factual)

B 19. Which of the following involves general and pervasive worries and fears?
a. conduct disorder
b. overanxious disorder
c. separation anxiety disorder
d. anorexia nervosa
(Objective 8, Conceptual)

C 20. Research has shown that anxiety disorders:

a. are as frequent as conduct disorders
b. are not likely to show spontaneous remission
c. seem to be caused by factors in the family environment
d. are largely caused by biological factors
(Objective 8, Factual)

D A 21. Anorexia nervosa is:

a. an anxiety disorder
b. frequently accompanied by bulimia
c. primarily a disorder that affects adolescents and young adults
d. an eating disorder
(Objective 9, Conceptual)

D 22. Research findings about anorexia indicate that:

a. the parents expect the child to be perfect
b. the parents demand absolute compliance
c. the person asserts autonomy by controlling how much she or he eats
d. all of the above
(Objective 9, Factual)

D 23. A difference between anorexia and depression is that depressed people:

a. are hopeless
b. have feelings of low self-worth
c. are helpless
d. are lethargic and unmotivated

(Objective 10, Factual)

C D 24. Studies about childhood depression indicate that:

a. biological theories are not helpful in explaining depression
b. the existence of this disorder before adolescence is unclear
c. childhood depression may be related to severe emotional neglect
d. all of the above

(Objective 10, Factual)

ESSAY QUESTION

1. A variety of models have been used to study and explain child psychopathology and to guide treatment efforts. Explain what a child psychopathology model is, identify the major models of child psychopathology, and indicate how they are different from one another.

Biological
medical
neurological
Genetic

Environmental
Sociological
Psychodynamic
Behavioral models.
Family

ANSWER KEYS

Matching

1. e 2. m 3. i 4. h 5. a 6. l 7. d 8. n

9. c 10. k 11. g 12. o 13. b 14. f 15. j

Multiple Choice

1. c (p. 580)	13. d (p. 592)
2. a (p. 580)	14. c (p. 593)
3. b (p. 581)	15. a (p. 593)
4. c (p. 581)	16. d (pp. 594-595)
5. b (p. 582)	17. b (p. 596)
6. a (p. 584)	18. a (p. 598)
7. d (p. 585)	19. b (p. 599)
8. d (p. 586)	20. c (p. 600)
9. c (p. 587)	21. d (pp. 600-601)
10. d (pp. 588-590)	22. d (pp. 601-602)
11. a (p. 591)	23. d (p. 602)
12. b (p. 591)	24. c (pp. 603-604)

Essay Question

1. A model is a a set of ideas and assumptions about the causes of some event or condition. There are different models for understanding psychopathology. They differ in placing greater emphasis on biological or environmental factors and in the extent to which they take developmental factors into account. Biological models include the medical model, neurological and physiological models, and genetic models. Sociological models, behavioral models, psychodynamic models, and family models place primary emphasis on environmental factors as causes of child psychopathology. The developmental model emphasizes interaction between biological and environmental factors and also the role of development and the child's age when trying to explain the origin of child psychopathology. **(pp. 580-590)**